Transcripts of Meetings 1941–1946

Book Studio London 2009
ISBN 978-0-9559090-5-4
Second Edition

ACKNOWLEDGEMENTS

Gratitude to Janet Flanner and Solita Solano for donating their papers to the Library of Congress and dedicating them to the public, to George Adie for carefully retaining the transcript of meeting fifteen and to Joseph Azize for translating it from the French into English.

CONTENTS

Question: Something intolerable happens in my work. In spite of my efforts I cannot remember myself; to get a better quality. It's useless to set myself hours of work by the clock. I get no result. Why?

Gurdjieff: That comes from your egoism. Particularly big egoism in which you have lived till now. You are enclosed in it; you must get out of it. To get out, you must learn to work. Not only for yourself alone, but for others. You began with work on your parents. You must change your task. Take a new one, the same one on the neighbour, no matter who, all beings, or choose from the people amongst you. You must work for yourself through the aim of being able to help them. This alone will struggle against egoism. I see that you both have a very bad past, a particular egoism. All the old material comes to the fore. That is why you can do nothing. It is normal; according to order, according to law. Before attaining the aim, there are many ascents and descents. This should reassure you. I could reassure you completely, but you must work yourself.

Question: To get out of this state of suffering, so vivid and so negative. (Two kinds of suffering, one objective, one subjective.) Can I make use of exterior means, take opium for instance?

Gurdjieff: No, you must work on yourself. Destroy the egoism in which you have always lived. Try what I say. Change your task. It is necessary now to reach a new stage. Both of you are on the way to the Gare de Lyon, but you go by different routes, one by London and one by the Opera. You are both at about the same distance.

Question: I see my powerlessness and my cowardice. I can say nothing and do nothing for another. Because my head is not clear. I have a sensation of whether a thing is right or not, but I cannot explain why clearly.

Gurdjieff: You cannot say anything or do anything for another. You do not know what you need for yourself, you cannot know what he needs. Work with purpose for him. But play your role. Be apart internally: See. Externally speak as he does, so as not to hurt him. You must acquire the force to do this. Play a role. Become double. For the present you work as overseer. Do what I tell you, you cannot

1

do more. Love of your neighbour; that is the *Way*. Bring to everyone that which you felt for your parents.

Question: From the beginning of the work, one has this desire.

Gurdjieff: Certainly, it is the same thing; always the same thing that returns in a different degree. Now another degree. You must overcome this crisis. Everything comes from false love of oneself, of the opinion one has of oneself, which is lies.

Question: Everything has been turned upside down in me by the exercise—in all my work. It has taken away the joy of the work, has made it painful, without hope, I feel like a donkey pulling a very heavy cart up a hill.

Gurdjieff: It is because in you are other parts which are touched. It is like a painter who always mixes the same colours and there is never any red. When he puts red in, it changes everything. You must continue.

Question: This exercise has made me feel something which is new for me; when I try to do it and put my attention on this small motionless point and see that I cannot hold myself in front of it, I have a sensation of my nothingness and I seem to understand humility better. This small point is greater than I.

Gurdjieff: Because you have a dog in yourself which hinders you in everything. It is called insolence towards oneself. You must destroy this dog. Afterwards you will feel master of this point, that you are stronger and it is nothing. I have no confidence in the artistic type which lives in the imagination, has ideas behind its head, not inside, thinks it feels and experiences, but in reality is only occupied with exterior things. It lives only on the surface, outside, not inside, not in itself. Artists know nothing of reality and imagine that they know. Do not trust yourself. Enter into yourself, all parts of yourself. Absolutely necessary to learn to feel and think at the same time in everything that you do, in every day life. You are an empty person.

Question: How should one pray?

Gurdjieff: I will explain, but it is for later. In our solar system certain substances emanate from the sun and the planets, in the same way as those emanated by the earth, making contact at certain points in the solar system. And these points can reflect themselves in materialised images which are the inverted images of the All

Highest—the Absolute. I tell you that there always exists a material-ised image in our atmosphere. If people could have enough concentration to enter into contact with this image, they would receive this substance; thereby receiving, and establishing a telepathic line like the telephone.

Question: Do these images materialise in human form?

Gurdjieff: Yes.

Question: If someone puts himself in touch with this image, and a second person can put himself in touch with him, and a third and a fourth, can they all receive this image?

Gurdjieff: If seven persons can concentrate enough to put themselves in touch with this image, they can communicate, at any distance, by the line between them and the seven form one. They can help each other. By the way, it is only by explaining something to others that one understands and assimilates oneself completely.

Question: I want to know if by materialising the image of a saint, this will get me what I particularly desire.

Gurdjieff: You think like an ordinary person. You have not the means of materialising anything now. For the present take a task of auto-suggestion, so that one part convinces the other and repeats and repeats to it what you have decided. There is a series of seven exercises for the successive development of the seven centres. We cite the first, the brain, the one which counts in ordinary life. (The head is a luxury.) The other, the emotional also; but the only one which is necessary is the spinal cord, the one which you must first develop and strengthen. This exercise will strengthen it. Hold out both arms horizontally at an exact angle, at the same time looking fixedly at a point before you. Divide your attention exactly between point and arms. You will find that there are no associations, no place for them, so occupied you will be with point and position of arms. Do this sitting down, standing, then on knees. Twenty-five minutes each position, several times a day—or fewer. Once I had a pupil who could stay for two hours without moving his arms one centimetre. For other things he was nothingness.

Question: When I wish to make such efforts for work, a hard barrier forms in my chest, impossible to overcome. What should I do?

Gurdjieff: It is nothing. You are not in habit of using this centre—it is a muscle which contracts—just muscular. Continue, continue.

Question: I have done this exercise till I had aching shoulders. While doing it, I had the sensation of "I." I felt myself apart, really "I."

Gurdjieff: You cannot have "I." "I" is very expensive thing. You are cheap. Do not philosophise, it does not interest me, and do not speak of "I." Do the exercise as service, as an obligation, not for results (like "I"). Results will come later. Today it is only service. Only that is real.

Question: I feel more within myself, but as if I were before a closed door.

Gurdjieff: It is not one door but many doors. You must open each door, learn to.

Question: I have worked especially on self-love.

Gurdjieff: Without self-love a man can do nothing. There are two qualities of self-love. One is a dirty thing, the other, an impulse, love of the real "I." Without this, it is impossible to move. An ancient Hindu saying—"Happy is he who loves himself, for he can love me." I see from Mme de Salzmann's report that no one has understood me. One needs fire. Without fire, there will never be anything. This fire is suffering, voluntary suffering, without which it is impossible to create anything. One must prepare, must know what will make one suffer and when it is there, make use of it. Only you can prepare, only you know what makes you suffer, makes the fire which cooks, cements, crystallises, *does*. Suffer by your defects, in your pride, in your egoism. Remind yourself of the aim. Without prepared suffering there is nothing, for by as much as one is conscious, there is no more suffering. No further process, nothing. That is why with your conscience you must prepare what is necessary. You owe to nature. The food you eat which nourishes your life. You must pay for these cosmic substances. You have a debt, an obligation, to repay by conscious work. Do not eat like an animal but render to nature for what she has given you, nature, your mother. Work—a drop, a drop, a drop—accumulated during days, months, years, centuries, perhaps will give results.

Question: I've arrived at the point where I am very unhappy, everything is distasteful to me, of no interest.

Gurdjieff: And that handkerchief arranged like that in your pocket? That interests you. Well, nature wishes you well, I am glad. She brings you to real work by making all the rest distasteful—it's a certain crossing you must make, the more you work, the more you will come out of this discomfort, this emptiness, this lack.

Question: Even work is distasteful to me.

Mme de Salzmann: Because you do not work. There is never any work with you, nothing ever between us when we are together—it is empty. One person cannot carry everything alone. You must make the effort for yourself. Tonight it is the same. Nobody is there—nobody makes the effort.

Gurdjieff: Then one must change the way of working. Instead of accumulating during one hour, one must try to keep constantly the organic sensation of the body. Sense one's body again, continually without interrupting one's ordinary occupations—to keep a little energy, to take the habit, I thought the exercises would allow you to keep the energy a long time, but I see it is not so. Wet a handkerchief, wring it out, put it on your skin. The contact will remind you. When it is dry, begin again. *The key to everything—remain apart.* Our aim is to have constantly a sensation of oneself, of one's individuality, this sensation cannot be expressed intellectually, because it is organic. It is something which makes you independent when you are with other people.

Lanctin: I am not able to stop associations while I work.

Gurdjieff: It is necessary to prepare before the exercise of trying to see with three parts.

Aboulker: At the beginning when I was working, I felt in myself an emotion. Now I cannot find it any more. I have a constant sensation of dryness. Yesterday this warmer feeling came back, but much weaker.

Gurdjieff: It is the sign of a crisis. It is because you have arrived at mi. You must pass this interval by yourself and find in yourself the necessary strength. Your head, which is as though separated from you, must help you.

Lanctin: How?

Gurdjieff: It must convince you. It must allow you to see yesterday and tomorrow.

Lanctin: But my head is weak.

Gurdjieff: Yes, but without your head you also would be weak. It is necessary to use it in this way.

Simone: A little while ago I started to read again, but I find in myself that which has always prevented me from working, a sort of avidity which leaves me at the end of a short time tired and having retained nothing. My time has been wasted.

Gurdjieff: It is because you only read with your head. Do an exercise. Read only a little—a page at a time. At first you must try to understand with your head, then to feel, then to experience. And then come back and think. Exercise yourself to read with your three centres. In each book there is material for enriching oneself. It doesn't matter what you read and it doesn't matter the quantity, but the quality of the way of reading.

Pauline: Following a shock, I have really seen what has been my life—empty, sterile, useless. And I don't want to lose this vision, this feeling. Otherwise, I feel that I will fall again and again lose my life.

Gurdjieff: Cosmic phenomena for which you are not responsible go against your work. You can only give yourself your word that when life becomes quiet, you will set yourself to work.

Mechin: I feel that my intellectual centre is different and that I do

6

not find in myself any affirming force. What can I do?

Gurdjieff: There is there a little secret. It is that you are a big egoist. You only know yourself. You have no responsibility. It is because of that that you lack this affirmative force. For everything that you have, everything that constitutes you, you are under obligation, and you must repay for all this, so that then other things may be given to you. But instead of this, you are astonished not to have received even more.

Solange: I am not able to sense myself. What can I do to get a sensation of myself?

Gurdjieff: Only your head wishes to remember. Your effort is theoretical. You must establish a contact between your head and your body. Place one leg in iced water and leave it there, trying to establish this contact. Then do the same with the other leg. (It is too early to come here.)

Lebeau: Since the time that you advised me to be egoistical, I have done it. But I constate in myself a desire to live only in this better part—I would like to stay there always and ignore all the rest. I feel a great laziness invading me in relation to external life, and the smallest thing is for me a great effort.

Gurdjieff: It is very good that this state appears in you. This proves that later you will truly become someone responsible, like a man, and I love you in advance for this. But now it is necessary to struggle without rest. You must maintain a constant conflict between this state and your understanding. The more you wish to do nothing, the more you must make yourself do. You must struggle unmercifully and it is a struggle which will produce in you the necessary substance that you may, with my help, create in yourself a real "I."

Simone: I see how I am always beaten by my functions. My habits form an automatism which is in me like a block on which I can get no hold. On one side I have my work, and on the other my life, in which nothing changes.

Gurdjieff: We have already often said that if one develops one side, the other will develop also. One must struggle.

Simone: But rightly. I am not able to have a conflict in myself.

Gurdjieff: Because you do not do. In order to take for oneself everything from this table, you have to go over the table. Otherwise you will never be able to go further. You can continue to live like this ten years, a thousand years. You will never change. Even God, if he wished it, would not be able to help you. He would not have the right . . . Only you yourself can struggle against your laziness. There are two tendencies in you. But you, you sleep. It is necessary for you to get up and fight.

Simone: Is this laziness born in me or acquired?

Gurdjieff: I think that it is a natural tendency. The more your psyche wishes a certain thing, the more the body refuses. Perhaps it has been placed there by nature, so that there should be a struggle. Moreover, it is a good thing. These are conditions of work. If it did not exist, it would be necessary to place something in you, in order to replace it. It is also a factor for remembering. Each time that you feel it, you must think about your work. It is also a good thing that you see your laziness, because many people are lazy, but they do not see it.

Simone: I have known it for fifteen years, but I haven't made any headway against it.

Gurdjieff: What did you do then? You were sorry about it. But in this way in a hundred years nothing will change. There is no reason for it to change—only if you set yourself to struggle conscientiously.

Gabrielle: I need help, because I am going through a very profound crisis and I have even lost the taste of work. When I wish to work, I fall into a leaden sleep.

Gurdjieff: Something is preparing itself in you, but you do not see it, and the work must be more and more painful for you, since you have less and less contact with yourself. In spite of this, you must continue to force yourself. You must take this step by yourself. Think that it is not only for you that you work, and that perhaps (and it is absolutely true in a proportion of ten percent) the future fate of others depends on it, is tied to yours.

Louise: I am asking for help because I am no longer able to work. All these bad interior things are there again. I have an intense desire to work, to remember myself, but I am unable to do it. My body no longer obeys me. It is the body which is master.

Gurdjieff: I am very happy, for you, because this state is objectively good. Keep going. In a few days I will give you some help.

Lebeau: Can one work in a Turkish bath and what is best to do?

Gurdjieff: The "hammam" is an excellent place for work if one can work there. (Particularly when one is in the warmest room or between the hands of the masseur.) Self-remember without ceasing. Even do exercises there.

[Tracol says that he fears here especially imagination in the work. Mr. Gurdjieff replies to him that even in this case it would not be very dangerous because the time passed there is short.]

In order to be able to work there give yourself your word before going there. Think while there. Set yourself a task because in the beginning it is difficult; however if one succeeds, one can do some excellent work there. Animalism expands, one is completely inside his agreeable corporal sensations and to work here offers difficulties.

Philippe: How does one understand the words: "sacrifice thy suffering"?

Gurdjieff: First, where do these words come from? [From a talk with Mr. Gurdjieff.] Sacrifice your suffering for your neighbour, your voluntary suffering, not for yourself, but for others. This rule used to form part of the oath pronounced formerly by doctors when they were astrologers and a long time ago when they had to promise to sacrifice their sleep, their fatigue, their suffering, for others.

Philippe: Why does the major part of human suffering revolve around love and things of sex?

Gurdjieff: Why this question? It does not concern you personally. Ask it in another way.

Philippe: Why are the major part of the associations, which interfere with the work, sexual associations?

Gurdjieff: This question is subjective. It is not so for all men. It is an abnormality which is a result of infantile masturbation. But what is the connection between this and suffering. There is no trace of suffering here. Each man has in him three excrements which elaborate themselves and which must be rejected. The first is the result of ordinary nourishment and eliminates itself naturally, and this must be each day, otherwise there follow all sorts of illnesses.

(The physician knows this well.) For the same reason that you go to the bathroom for this maintenance, you must go to the bathroom for the second excrement which is rejected from you by the sexual function. It is necessary for health and the equilibrium of the body; and certainly it is necessary in some to do it each day, in others each week, in others again every month or every six months. It is subjective. For this you must choose a proper bathroom. One that is good for you. A third excrement is formed in the head; it is rubbish of the food impressions, and the wastes accumulate in the brain. (The physician ignores it, just as he ignores the important role of the appendix in digestion, and rejects it as wastes.)

It is not necessary to mingle the acts of sex with sentiment. It is sometimes abnormal to make them coincide. The sexual act is a function. One can regard it as external to oneself, although love is internal. Love is love. It has no need of sex. It can be felt for a person of the same sex, for an animal even, and the sexual function is not mixed up there. Sometimes it is normal to unite them; this corresponds to one of the aspects of love. It is easier to love this way. But at the same time it is then difficult to remain impartial as love demands. Likewise if one considers the sexual function as necessary medically, why would one love a remedy, a medicine? The sexual act originally must have been performed only for the purpose of reproduction of the species, but little by little men have made of it a means of pleasure. It must have been a sacred act. One must know that this divine seed, the Sperm, has another function, that of the construction of a second body in us, from whence the sentence: "Happy he who understands the function of the 'eccioeccari' for the transformation of his being. Unhappy he who uses them in a unilateral manner."

Aboulker: Why do religions forbid the sexual act?

Gurdjieff: Because originally we knew the use of this substance, whence the chasteness of the monks. Now we have forgotten this knowledge and only remains the prohibition which attracts to the monks quantities of specific disorders and illnesses. Look at the priests where they grow "fat like pigs," (the concern about eating dominating them) or they are "skinny as the devil" (and they have inside little love for their neighbour), the fat are less dangerous and more gentle.

Lanctin: You have advised me to read, to collect information, but what to begin with? Shouldn't I work on certain things before others?

Gurdjieff: What is important is to gather the soul of things, the spirit and not the form. Forget the words, the details; this is nothing; but keep in yourself the substance, what is behind. It is this that you must accumulate in yourself. It is this which, depositing itself in you, will create little by little a subjective understanding which will really be yours. *[To Philippe]* For example, in what you write, amongst all those words, all the useless, all that which objectively has no value, perhaps there is one small flash of diamond—it is that which you have to search for, collect and accumulate in yourself.

Louise Lacaze: I do not know what is the most important thing to do in myself, on what I must put my efforts.

Gurdjieff: Since you have been coming here, you always hear repeated that you must acquire an "I." Actually, everything in you is in a state of change, unstable, inconsistent. You are the carriage with many chance passengers. You must acquire an unchangeable "I." This is the most important thing, on which you must put all your efforts.

Philippe: Since I have known you, I have experienced many feelings. Now I hate all these feelings. I would like to be able to experience one right feeling. If I say this, it is because I feel myself that I am coming nearer to it.

Gurdjieff: Now I must entertain the idea that you can be a comrade to me. Up till now, inwardly I was indifferent to you, outwardly I considered you thus and thus, but nothing inwardly. First, you must become my "comrade," so that later on, much later, you may become "brother." Now I say "comrade" and not "brother."

Luc: A few days ago, when I was remembering myself, so that I could make a decision which was important for me, suddenly I had a feeling of the unreality of my life, and at the same time the unreality of all my good moments. But nevertheless, I felt it was the best that I have had and that, at the same time, they all had something in common. In the same way I noticed that time no longer existed in my memory, that things of childhood were the same as things much more recent. (I experience the same feeling.)

Gurdjieff: You have grown inwardly, but what has developed is weak. It is necessary to nourish it, either with interior or exterior material. But you have interior material, material of information. According to whether this thing which is formed in you is heavier or lighter, it comes out or enters into you. It rises and falls according to it's weight. Perhaps only he is my real pupil who, at every moment when he says "I am" feels it resound in the same place in him—he who feels himself to be the same at all these moments.

Kahn: I would like to know if this thing which I feel in myself side by side with my work, this love that I would like to see become the essence of my essence, which seems to me to come from something other than my work and my efforts, must I push it away—must I not believe in it, and hold strictly to the work that Mr. Gurdjieff has indicated?

Gurdjieff: Yes, you must do exactly what you have been told to do and nothing else. You have not yet arrived at the place on the way when you can listen to those things. All these are temptations on your way. Push them away and do your work strictly.

Simone: I feel that I must introduce in my task, in my work, a person close to me, but what adds to the difficulty is that I feel in this person weaknesses similar to my own, and my weaknesses reinforce hers and her weaknesses reinforce mine. I don't know how to defend myself against this and what attitude to take.

Gurdjieff: You must pay no attention to the exterior. This is exterior. You must only know your task and do it interiorly. The other person, consciously or not, plays her role, acts her character. You do not know her, you do not know who she is, whether it is Moses, or some other person. It is not important. What is important for you is your inner task.

S: I am very often deceived in my opinion of others. That is bad for me. I give people credit for qualities they do not possess; and as for the people who do possess them, I see it only later when I know them better. I don't know how to detect hypocrisy and I'm always seeing it too late. I would like to have a means of judging people and recognising who can be useful to me and who is useless.

Gurdjieff: You cannot, you must first prepare yourself to see reality. While waiting, play a role exteriorly. Interiorly, recognise your nonentityness. You don't know anything. If you have the habit of doing things in a certain way, do them in this way. Say "Good morning" as you always say good morning. But at the same time work to keep up with the work we're doing here and then you'll be able to recognise people. At present, everyone is like you: nothing, zero. Whether he be a workman, or a senator, he is *merde* like you. Get to work at not being a nonentity; work, so that in a day, a month or a year you will not be a nonentity. Do everything exactly as you are accustomed to doing. But you must play a role, without participating, without identifying yourself interiorly; and remember what your value is—nothing. Work, work and again work, in order to change that nothingness into something definite.

Education makes a mask. When you see people, you believe in this mask. After a while the mask falls and you see that they are the same *merde* as yourself. No matter whom you see, he represents a mask. If you look at him longer, with impartiality and attention, you see that he is not always able to keep his mask; at the same moment, the *merde* will show through. It is the same which is in you. He is nothing, as you are nothing, even if he is a colonel, senator or millionaire. It's only the combinations of life that are there. His grandfather was like that, his father was like this, and he profits from it. But he himself represents only nothingness.

Only he is not a nothing who has understood his nothingness and has worked on himself to change it. That man is another quality of *merde*: with "roses." It is still *merde* but it has not the same odour.

Work, put everything towards it, and be sure that all who do not work are nothings like you. You are nothing, but he also is nothing.

He is a general, a colonel, these are exterior things: they cost nothing.

In life, everything is accidental—occupations, position, all obligations; whether one is the mayor or the corner policeman. It is life which creates these abnormalities. Interiorly, everything is always the same thing. Exterior things do not change the interior things. Only conscious work is able to change the interior—conscious labour and voluntary suffering.

Sim: I have noticed for a long time that very often, and concerning very different matters, an interior voice told me what I had to do. I perceived it, I heard what it said, but without acting on what it told me. I have acted otherwise and afterwards I see the voice is always right. I would like to know if I should pay no attention to it or on the contrary follow it more?

Gurdjieff: Do nothing about all that. Buy a little notebook. Make a record. Write down, but do nothing. That voice is your instinct; sometimes instinct can appear through the consciousness, but it is rare. Perhaps it will prove that you have true instinct. See if your records will show that. Now perhaps we will find an exercise. But do nothing before.

Sim: But to write it, I will have to do it actually [realizer].

Gurdjieff: Make a note, I will speak afterwards. Perhaps it's suggestibility, fantasy, idiocy. According to the result, I shall say what it is mathematically. Sometimes instinct is a very independent thing. But as for you, I don't know. I will speak afterwards. Before that, continue as you are doing, before you noticed anything.

Sim: It would have been better lately if I had done what it told me.

Gurdjieff: We shall see. You think that, but perhaps it's the contrary. Perhaps it's psychopathic. I do not wish to believe anything except the facts given by the records [statistique]. You speak subjectively. The objective I do not know.

Lu: I try to maintain the feeling of nonentityness and voluntary suffering as often as possible. But I notice it gives a paralysis as far as action is concerned. It shows the futility of all action and busyness. If, before I had to make an effort to do a given thing, today I must also carry the iron collar of this nonentityness. The effort is doubled. What shall I do so that this feeling of nullity does not paralyse me, does not interfere with exterior life?

Gurdjieff: Do as I have already told you. One must work only the third part of one's waking state. Make a special time for the work. Don't mix things; fix a time tomorrow between ten and eleven o'clock, ordinary life. The other ideas, the work, send them to the devil.

Lu: One is no longer free to drive away the feeling of one's nothingness.

Gurdjieff: Put aside your new state. And do as you did before, when you hadn't begun to work. One must never mix matters. Do not yet use the results of the interior work for exterior work. Not yet. You are at school, like a child. It isn't for life, not for earning money. You would know a great secret which you should not use. That is one thing, life is another thing. Wednesday, Friday, Sunday, you do what you like; send to the devil all other thoughts. If you mix them, one will impede the other.

Lu: The feeling of nullity, uncalled, which comes by itself, is indeed automatic and therefore destructive.

Gurdjieff: In the time set aside for the work, make a comment more lively. The rest of the time, to the devil. It is psychopathy.

Gurdjieff [to An.]: I have never heard the sound of your voice. I know your voice in life, but not here in our circle. Can you say anything to me?

An: I haven't worked enough yet to ask a question.

Gurdjieff: How do you know that?

An: Because I do not dare.

Gurdjieff: Then you do have a question.

An: Not today.

Gurdjieff: Well, then, yesterday.

[Mme de Salzmann tells Gurdjieff what questions An. has asked her.]

Gurdjieff: He who works becomes an actor, a real actor in life. To be an actor is to play a role. Life is a theatre where every man plays a role. Every day they change it. Today one role, tomorrow another role. He only is a good actor who is able to remember himself and consciously play his role, no matter what it may be.

An: But how does one know the role one must play?

Gurdjieff: You speak with Boussique—you know who she is, how one must be with her, what she likes. Well then do it. Interiorly she is nothing for me, she is *merde* for me. She likes people to kiss her hand; I do it because she likes that. I am kind to her. Interiorly I want to insult her, but I don't do it. I play my role. So then she becomes my slave. Interiorly I don't react.

An: I don't succeed in being good to others.

Gurdjieff: Perhaps you are not yet free.

An: I wish to profit from everything egoistically for myself.

Gurdjieff: You must work. Kill the dogs in you. You only play your role theoretically, but very quickly you forget and you return to your nothingness. Your task will be to remember longer.

Dr. Ab: What good is it to have slaves?

Gurdjieff: For life; if you haven't any slaves, you are the slave of someone.

Dr. Ab: Cannot everyone simply be equal?

Gurdjieff: Never. How is it possible? You have four eyes and I two. Already there is a difference. Your father loved your mother if he was lying to the left; my father loved my mother if he were lying on the right. The results I am one, you another. For me one law, for you another. The well-being of man is that everyone be his slaves. You say that the work has changed you. Thanks to the work you are no longer a *merde;* thanks to conscious labours and voluntary suffering. Objectively you deserve it.

Dr. Be: At present our dogs oblige us to use others for our ends.

Gurdjieff: There you have good ground for being-work. Today you are an ordinary man; in your work try to be a superior man. Afterwards perhaps you will be a complete man, a real man. At the moment when you feel your dogs, struggle against them; this conflict is necessary for you in order to become a real man, it's good soil for the work. And there are still more dogs in you that are invisible.

Dr. Be: But shouldn't one give up using egoistically one's power over others?

Gurdjieff: Today you do it unconsciously; try to do it consciously. Then it will be good, both for them and for you. There is no other justice.

[Reading of chapter on Ashiata Shiemash—Dinner—After dinner.]
[A. turns towards Mr. Gurdjieff and asks]: Mr. Gurdjieff, may I ask a question?
Gurdjieff: I have been Mr. Gurdjieff for a long time. What do you want to ask me?
A: Since I came to the work I have learned many things but I have been able to put nothing into practice. I have tried several times but I get no result, real results which would satisfy me. And now, during the holidays, I would like to try something, the main thing on which I could hang my work.
Gurdjieff: You expect results and you take no measures. What do you wish? Have you a measure? *[To the others]* She says she works and that she does nothing.
A: I would like to know something. It would be necessary for me to work to have a satisfactory result. For instance, in the remembering, negative conditions, identifications; I get no results with all that. I try to do everything together. I would like to work on just one thing.
Gurdjieff: For you if you are going on a holiday this is a good question as I understand it. I regret one thing. There is an aspect of you which I do not know. I know five aspects; two I do not know.
[Mme de Salzmann speaks to Mr. Gurdjieff in Russian.]
Gurdjieff: You are going away for a long time?
A: Four or five weeks.
Gurdjieff: Then you have a long time. I am going to give you a very original exercise. Many people here can even be astonished. I am going to give you a task. After you have done it we will talk. This is a very big thing and impossible to do in four or five weeks. It needs four or five months, perhaps longer. Only I can explain it now. This is a very original task. I am sure that if you do it you will receive what you are waiting for. You deserve, you have every right to the results of this exercise. Only this complicated thing cannot come quickly. During the holidays do the ground work for it. "*I am*," that you understand. Now meditate on the subject of this exercise. "I wish that whoever looks on me may feel love and respect for me and

18

I wish above all that the desire to help me may appear in that person, (and at the same time as you breathe you say '*I am*'), and in everything that I think I wish truly to be like that." If you do that honestly, consciously, as a service, I answer for a result in six months. This exercise is your God, more than your father or your mother. Do it until I tell you it's enough.

A: How many times must it be done, I mean how many times a day?

Gurdjieff: All the time if you can. But you forget, you cannot. Do it two or three times in each twenty-four hours. When you wake up, when you go to sleep and in the middle of the day before lunch or dinner. You fix three periods for this exercise. If, between whiles, you remember it, even automatically—then do it. No danger in that. This should be your all—more than God, more than everybody. Do nothing else. Don't manipulate no wiseacreing, no philosophising. Do this exercise as a service, as an obligation, as if you were going to make money by doing it. When you return then I will speak to you as to how to continue. Nobody astonished?

[A long silence.]

P: May I ask a question, sir? There is one thing which has preoccupied me for a long time. How should a man act towards a woman so as to be her master and make her happy? To be really master of the situation.

Gurdjieff: Your question is, what is it necessary to do. First of all you must be a man inside yourself. Every woman should feel herself a man's slave. This is the property of women, they are made that way. For that there is a law. You ought to represent the boss, the master. You should consider all things as the master. If you are like that, she, without manipulation, without anything, (it always happens) becomes your slave. Without explanations or anything, it only depends on you. If I am a man I will have a woman. This depends on what I am, what you are. If I ought to have seven wives all seven will be my slaves, perhaps because I am a man. Not only will all seven be unable to deceive me but they will tremble at the mere idea of deceiving me; they feel that they have a master. These seven women always and everywhere are my slaves. This, firstly, is what is necessary. Now secondly many other things are still necessary. What I have just said is the main thing. Now I say secondly: You are man, she is woman. Nature has given you more possibilities than to woman. You have more physical strength; everything you have more than her. Amongst all these things you have more logical thought than the woman. You should first prepare her, calm her, put her into a certain state and then logically explain to her what can happen for the future. Show her life not for today but life in a month, in a year, in five years time. As it is established on earth that if husband and wife live well together they will live a long time together, and as life is long it is necessary to explain to her what things she must not do and what she must do. If you explain to her as I have told you, she will do it.

P: One must not be angry, never negative?

Gurdjieff: You must be the opposite. Science says a woman is hysterical, she has five Fridays in one week. Man, a real man, has one Friday. Science of all epochs explains this. If you are not master of your state you do not know which Friday she has today. What you have decided, put that into her. You tell her. Even if she is at Friday number three, do the same number four or number five—do the same. If you continue a hundred times, a thousand times, she will transform herself and will receive that which you wish. You are obliged to be a man; she is obliged to fulfil her obligations as a woman. You cannot be egoist. You are a man. You ought to demand of her that she be woman. If the man is an egoist, he is merde. He wants to do everything (as it pleases him, by chance) and he expects his wife to be a woman?

Little by little it can happen that she may reach the same state as him; either nature does it or it becomes established by force of law. Begin at the beginning. If she has five Fridays a week and if you, not being a man, have two or even three Fridays in a week, first of all, try, like any normal person to have only one Friday each week. When you succeed in having only one Friday, she too will have only one Saturday. Logical thought even automatically makes understandable the present, past, future and the rest. The man must be a man. Your question is very original and characteristic for everybody. A man can demand everything of his wife but he can only demand if he is, in truth, a man. If he is a man of the middle sex it is impossible. This, by the way, exists in all languages: there are two kinds of prostitutes: prostitutes in skirts and prostitutes in trousers. In trousers it is neither man nor woman—middle sex. He who always in his waking state is a man can never belong to the middle sex. Whether it be his mother, his sister or his wife, she will act as she is told to. Woman does not depend upon herself. If you are not a man then you are a prostitute and you suggest to her that which she is. You are half a man.

[All fall silent.]

Mme L: Sir, I experience great difficulty, whether here or with those who are near me, in explaining ideas and feelings. This is a real paralysis. It is very important for me. What can I do to free myself from this?

Gurdjieff: Necessary to be impartial. This is for you only. (People must never do that which I indicate for one person only.) You are you. You wish to work, you want to have an "I," a real "I." Your aim is *"I am,"* independent. *I am.* Now if you do not yet have it you imagine that you have it already. He who has an "I" is impartial towards all outside things. For everybody else he is impartial. For instance P is mad: he is mad. Nature made him that way—Father, Grandfather—he is mad, but I am not annoyed because he is mad. I look on him as a madman, I have pity. That is what is called very impartial. You look on all P's manifestations in this way: what can be the manifestations of a mad man? There are different qualities. For instance one may hold his cigarette like this *[he puts the lighted end in his mouth];* a normal person can never do that. But I am not cross, I have pity.

Dr. A: There are two qualities of pity. One can have contemptuous pity.

Gurdjieff: You—*you* have this pity but I do not have it. Either I have pity or I don't. Either he is mad or he is insolent. If he is mad, I have pity. If he is insolent, I do that (a blow) and I smash his facade—if he is in a place where I can do it; that is if he is not mad, if he is insolent; if he is mad I at once give him everything he wants. If I see that he is insolent and that there are no police about, he will never forget me—he will have lost three or four teeth. But pity is necessary. Everybody has pity. If you look in detail, you will see that one part comes from heredity, another from education which has spoiled you and the third comes from the sins of youth which you have committed. These qualities: that which comes from heredity I have pity for; for the second I have half-pity, but the third I never forgive. I explain subjective things to you. But if you use these in your life, you will never deceive yourself. One part comes from heredity, the second from education, the third from your behaviour in youth.

L: Work in revealing two worlds to us has revealed to me two different kinds of time. First, that of the body in which we live, the time of disquiet, of fear. And the time of remembering when there is neither disquiet nor anguish. Everyone contains in himself an explosive force which can contain in a very small packet a second force richer than ten years of the life of the body—of sleep. In this time of work one has no fear of losing time. In my ordinary state I am afraid of losing time. I would like to know what time is?

[Mme de Salzmann translates to Mr. Gurdjieff what L. wanted to say.]

Gurdjieff: Enough—she did not translate everything—but sufficient for my explanation. You notice that there are two different times for you as there are two states—the ordinary state, the habitual state in life and that state in which you remember yourself. That makes two different times. One time to which you are used and another time when you come to 6 rue des Colonels Renard—the time in which you are used to understanding and receiving everything is the time of the Rue des Colonels Renard. Now, if your fear comes up in the second time, that is to say, if you are afraid, sooner or later, of losing your time, then measure time by your state *"I am";* for this time has a being, *I am.* With the head you say *"I am":* it must be felt with the entire presence in all gestures, and at once it will change. Cosmic time will have to run as will be necessary for you. You are you. Even cosmic laws submit to unity however small that unity may be.

L: Is it not a bad thing to feel such a difference between the two times?

Gurdjieff: They are different. This will help you to press on to do that which you did not do in your past. If you have the "disease of tomorrow" that will not help you. But you have understood about this disease. I advise you to take every measure to have the time of *"I am"* with the state of *"I am,"* not only theoretically when you remember yourself, but to the most concentrated with all of your

22

presence. This is, in truth, a good question. The man who knows not the difference does not know what time he has. For he who knows, it serves as reminding factor—ordinary time, or time as it passes at 6 rue des Colonels Renard. Do you understand? Have you understood what it is you have to do? Then do it. Later will come a question which I will explain in detail. Think about there being two times, work time and the time of ordinary man.

L: Can one have a foresight of the work in the recollections of one's childhood?

Gurdjieff: Verify the state that you have *with "I am"* and your state without "*I am.*" This is the measure. When you remember yourself—one quality—when you do not remember yourself—another. It is not necessary to have a special apparatus; you perhaps have a taste of I am—of the quality of feeling that you have.

L: This is perhaps theoretical, but I need something theoretical, some material on time. My head needs it.

Gurdjieff: Ask Mme de Salzmann to arrange for you to read specially the chapter on time. Impossible to explain it briefly. Time flows in a way proportionate to your associations. Time flows in a manner proportionate to your state, to the quantity of associations flowing. If you remember yourself time passes slowly. Whilst *I am* three hours have already passed and they seemed like five minutes. At other times it's just the opposite. I have been waiting four minutes for Blonde and I think it is three hours. I have made a rendezvous at the cafe—without looking at anything I believe three hours go by in five minutes. When I am with "*I am,*" the new time, objective time goes quickly. Yesterday you had a quantity of subjective time. Today it is also subjective but of another quality, something that you must deserve and win. If you don't do it you will be the same as yesterday.

Luc: That is what I wanted to know.

[Silence.]

Z: May I ask you a question? I think that to reach knowledge one must be able to deceive oneself, and often I lack the courage to deceive myself and I shut myself up in a room. I would like to know how to have the courage to fall into error and go forward towards knowledge.

Gurdjieff: For that not necessary big thing. If for instance you

know that you are zero, if you have understood that you are merde—
a nullity and if you do not wish to be merde and if that is your
starting point for knowledge, then you must risk—"That or nothing." If you have already felt that and that you can be something
other, then you risk nothing. Why are you afraid? You have nothing
to lose. Don't pity yourself. For me merde is cheap, one even pays to
have it taken away. And now, my dear guest, seriously, have you
understood my reply? Are you content with my reply to your first
question? Then take your cheque-book and write on the cover (not
inside—inside is without cover), but on the outside, to remind you—
one looks and one always remembers. Inside it is without resources.
But when the war is over, I will say to you look how much it adds up
to on the cover and write the total inside. There is a cosmic law—an
objective law which says that each satisfaction must be paid for by a
dissatisfaction. And each dissatisfaction a man must sooner or later
pay for by a satisfaction. What one sows, one reaps. To remind
himself a man writes on his cheque-book. There is a strong connection between cheque-book and these questions. Books, notebooks,
one loses and changes them. This doesn't change. When there will
be something you will be able to count me two, three, four zeros.
That depends on you. This is practical, this is life. I regret that T. has
not tabled a satisfaction. At once I would have put up a dissatisfaction. P., have you understood why very often I recall cheque-book?
Why, consciously, unconsciously, automatically I know how to
remind about cheque-book?

Simone: Before knowing the work, I was much more restless, because I felt bad things of which I thought I would never be able to rid myself. This kept up in me a restlessness, not constant perhaps, but very frequent. I have perceived that with the work, this passed, and I have felt calmer inside. I would like to find again my state of restlessness because this is lacking in me. What could I think or do in order to find it again?

Gurdjieff: Before you believed that you could succeed like that. With these results you can never do anything. You shall succeed only if you make an effort stronger than the ordinary. But you have not even the taste for it perhaps. You have already been here a long time; you are bound to understand what is effort. Self-effort. I am going to tell you a secret: self-effort is never possible all at once; a preparation is necessary. Struggle is necessary. Till one succeeds, one forgets, one remembers, one forgets, one remembers. But when you are seated, calm, you can think and begin to do; until now you still have made no effort.

Simone: That's why I ask the question. I am there and I feel too tranquil.

Gurdjieff: You imagine, you believe that you shall go directly to Paradise. No, here there must be efforts above the ordinary. For example, for this person *[he indicates a newcomer]* it is good enough for her, but you, you shall not go far with this. You must begin to make a super effort, and now, if you do not do it, it is because you do not have an aim. How can you stay calm? With the effort you are making today, you will never succeed. A normal person could not be calm.

Simone: It is just for that reason that this makes me restless.

Gurdjieff: It is necessary here to make efforts. You are accustomed to performing as before in life. Before, this want, now already it is not enough. The effort must strain all your muscles, all your nerves, all your brain even. A similar concentration must be yours. You should have been doing it for a long time. In the beginning, for a new person it is pardonable. For you, you have the taste for real work. You must realise it in your ordinary life. I am—always: I-am.

25

Never forget. Little by little your "I" shall make a contact with your essence. It is necessary to repeat it many times.

Aboulker: I have come to prefer violent emotions, rather than the habitual and passive inertia.

Gurdjieff: This does not exist for your real "me," active or passive. It depends on your state. The external things are indifferent. Remember sometimes, you think that it is negative, and it is perhaps the contrary. In order to have a material truth, do not think about your state. Do not philosophise; only observe; aim at your real "me."

Luc: I have made close to the same observations as the doctor. But this invites negative emotions to return more strongly. This week has been the best, because I have had some negative emotions. It is dangerous, it is real, devastation is possible, but I have had the taste of what can be a life.

Gurdjieff: Continue. But with the understanding that what you are accumulating is a substantial thing not only for the present, but for the future. This is very important. It is already time to think of remembering and at the same time of picturing to yourself in forms, not words, what is happening to you.

Luc: I was exhausted by my negative emotions even organically. Today, I have never felt so well, so animated.

Gurdjieff: Never have you had, previously, any liquid silver. You must feel that you have today some liquid silver.

Luc: One feels that the body is under pressure, that it is the theatre of such a struggle that it is going to break in pieces.

Gurdjieff: Remember, I said; man is not a pig, he cannot burst when he eats. The pig has a normal stomach; it cannot eat more than its stomach permits; it would burst; man is a scoundrel; he has a stomach of india rubber. He is worse than the pig; he gulps down, he gulps down without ever bursting. Not only the stomach, all the organs are of rubber. But little by little he has degenerated. Even the rubber, if one does not use it, shrinks. It is only if one restores it a thousand times bigger that he is like he must be. "Burst," it is a fantastic word. Only the pig can burst, man cannot. The pig has a normal stomach, he can burst. The stomach of man is of rubber, and all his organs. Continue without fear, if it is ten times more strong, so much the better; you shall go ten times faster here in my group.

Have no fear, you will not burst. It is imagination. How can one burst if one eats well? You are used to gulping down like a pig. Never do you eat well. Only now you begin to learn what is true eating. Do not be afraid. Continue and continue. Leave this sensation which creates that each time this expands; you are exactly like a child who has the hiccups, when it has eaten a great deal. Nature enlarges his stomach. A child can have the hiccups a thousand times. You are on the first time. Do not be afraid; you shall have them nine hundred and ninety-nine times more.

Mme Franc: I understand well the struggle against the negative emotions but what troubles me the most is a very light side of my character which jokes, even about my very misery. This prevents in me remorse and pity. How can I get rid of it?

Gurdjieff: This proves that you do not know what you are looking for. You interest yourself in these questions without partaking of your instinct. You have said it very well. I understand why you do not advance. I know the secret of why you stamp on the spot, one, two, one, two; up to now, your instinct was isolated. It never took part in your work. I shall give you a series of exercises. But you have understood what I explained. You have felt that your interior is never interested in these things for which we are working. Something in you remains apart; it looks. Another part in you does something else; you work without instinct. Everything works; head, feeling, except that which must. It has never done anything to change.

Hignette: I have tried to use the negative emotions. I have overcome them very well, but I have had the feeling of annihilating them, rather than converting them. I do not succeed in using them as a force. I suppress them.

Gurdjieff: You do not suppress them. What happens in you is another impulse which for a short time takes the place of the negative impulse. Thus aside, for a moment. But it is not destroyed. One must do many times "tchik," "tchik," in order to destroy them. You cannot ascertain that it is absent; but if you change states, you shall see that it functions more feebly. Thus, you have a programme of work. If you have understood, continue to extirpate, to chase away the impulses. But don't be tranquil. You do it serenely. This is another impulse which replaces, too feeble for you to perceive it;

and you imagine that you no longer have negative emotions. Only strong vibrations reach your consciousness.

Mechin: In the exercises, I am very troubled by associations. I can do nothing against them. What shall I do?

Gurdjieff: Associations are a part of our presence. If our presence had an aim, it would want something to happen. This proves that our presence has no aim. You have an aim only with one centre—(he wants to arrive at Paradise with dirty boots). One must with all one's presence have an aim and work for this goal. Not with one part, one centre only. I have associations; but they do not reach my consciousness. The circulation of the blood is also done all alone. It is an automatic function. It does not disturb me. It goes on night and day. There are associations also, as my heart working, and there are other functions; for example, I see, if I pay attention, like that which I have eaten travels. I can think about this all evening, each centimetre gives different sensations. Automatically you are occupied with this. You must have an aim, and leave at the side the organic functions. Not to hear them with, the consciousness, with the thought. One must learn to think impartially. Only this amount of effort will bring you to normal thought. The exercise that he must do, Mme de Salzmann can formulate.

Gurdjieff [to Ansi]: Have you understood?

Ansi: No.

Gurdjieff [to Luc]: Do you understand?

Luc: Yes

Gurdjieff: You explain to him; this shall be your task.

Ansi: I noticed that before, my negative emotions came most of all in my relations with people. I was violent and disagreeable when saying things to people. For some time I have been trying to struggle against this. But I fall into indifference and I do not know how to change my state.

Gurdjieff: It is not necessary to change; it is very well. In you is growing a re-appreciation of values. Before, you were interested in cheap things. And that which was not interesting had no value to you. Now what has value for you is that which was not interesting to you before. This is the reason.

Ansi: But I want to change.

Gurdjieff: Why? Already your state has changed. Before, you did not see that you were interested in things without value. More so now. Your state has changed.

Ansi: But if something wounds me, instead of being angry or offended, I am indifferent.

Gurdjieff: Normal; it is small, but normal. Before, you had your own love. It is cheap, it is an ordinary thing; now you have understood it. You see that it is idiotic, a nullity, an excrement; before, you did not know it. Today you see it; you are not angry. You see the manifestations of excrement. If it is like this, I am very content. Without wanting it, without knowing it, you have already advanced objectively, mechanically advanced. Soon, you can be our estimable comrade.

Lanctin: Is it possible in actual conditions to avoid a too inharmonic development of the body in regard to the general development?

Gurdjieff: For the physical development, there exist no seasons. Not political seasons. It is always necessary. You must educate your body with your head, consciously. It is very simple. Never allow it to do what it wants. You make it do everything contrary to that which it loves. It likes sugar, you do not give it any. One must inure it to struggle, you are always right when you resist your body. It is simple. Everything contrary; it is *so* that God created your body and your intellect. It is a very simple thing. For this it is not necessary to read. The programme is very simple. Under all conditions, in all political situations, man must educate his body to be submissive to him. Your personality can educate your body. He in which the body is strong and has the initiative over him, this one is null. He who has his body enslaved is intelligent. You understand what is meant by intelligent? Intelligent means he who directs his body. If the body directs, you are a nullity, a peasant—if you direct your body you are intelligent. Thus, choose what you want. Intelligent or peasant? If you want to be a peasant, let your body direct you. If you want to be intelligent, let your consciousness direct your body. The more you want to direct your body, the more it opposes you. And in resisting you, the more strength it gives you.

Question: I wish to ask about work and fatigue. It seems to me that there is a difference between efforts of work and automatic efforts. Exterior work takes our energy; the other work, on the contrary, should accumulate energy. But it is the opposite. One is very tired, one loses energy.

Gurdjieff: And in the meantime, you keep it. Consciously, you eat the electricity that you have in your body and you transform it. This constitutes your force. Not the same kind of fatigue. The fatigue from real work has a future; you are tired, that will give you a substantial result, recharge your accumulator. And if you continue, you accumulate a substantial substance which fills your accumulator (battery). The more you tire yourself, the more your organism elaborates this substance.

Question: Is it that fatigue is favourable or not to efforts of concentration?

Gurdjieff: If it is ordinary fatigue, it is not worthwhile to make the effort. It depends on the other accumulator. You will not be able to do even ordinary things. You will lose your final forces. But for another sort of fatigue there is another law: the more you give, the more you will receive.

Question: I have noticed that in the morning when I am rested, I cannot work. In the evening, on the contrary, after all the fatigue of the day, I am more successful.

Gurdjieff: Because one part of you is tired and because you work without that part. You work with one or two centres. You must work with all three. If one centre is tired, it does not take part in the work and you obtain no results. If you think you can work better at night, it is subjective; not worth anything; it is cheap.

Question: Can one sleep consciously—remain conscious during sleep.

Gurdjieff: It is possible, but not for you now. One can remember something so that it enters into you automatically. Auto-suggestion. One can suggest to oneself during sleep. Before being able to sleep consciously one must have a different quality of sleep. There are gradations. There are four kinds of sleep; one can sleep a sixth, a quarter, a half or completely. It depends on what your waking state has been. If you dream while you sleep, you only sleep half. You then need seven and a half hours' sleep. If you do not dream, four and a half hours are enough. It is the quality that is important. You sleep seven and a half hours. You take two hours to relax at night, two hours to contract again in the morning. That leaves you three and a half hours of sleep. You do not relax consciously but automatically, and that takes time. You can relax yourself consciously until you sleep while on the other hand you establish the necessary relation between your body and your consciousness. In the morning when you wake, do the same thing. Make a programme immediately, reflecting, suggesting to yourself the way in which you are determined to spend the day. Do the same work which you have thought about. Your activity will double itself. Make a real programme, not a fantasy. You must create the habit. You can do this only little by little. Nothing happens all at once. Change the quality of your sleep. Give yourself a good cold rubdown before you sleep. When you are going to sleep, pray for your near ones who are dead. These things are a good preparation for sleep. Otherwise, you will continue your dreams and fantasies of the evening.

[Two of those present say they cannot sleep on Thursdays, the day of the meetings for questions and answers. Mr. Gurdjieff addresses a third.]

Gurdjieff: Does this happen to you, doctor?

A: No, as soon as I close my eyes, I fall asleep.

Gurdjieff: Well, everyone is not a cousin like you. You know what I call a cousin of man. (Cow.)

Question: How can one acquire detachment?

Gurdjieff: One must have an ideal. Create an ideal for yourself. This will save you from automatic attachments. Think about this consciously and automatically this will grow and form a centre of gravity.

Question: Is it not easier to detach oneself from material things than from feelings?

Gurdjieff: All have the same value. You attach yourself with one centre or the other. You must look at this in this way, without philosophising. You have neither an ideal or a serious aim. You are a mechanism. You must have contact with something, but you have contact with nothing. So that everything has contacts with you—you are a slave. You must accustom yourself to prepare yourself for work. One certain time of day must he consecrated to work; you do nothing else. You sacrifice this. And if you cannot work yet, you do nothing. You *think* about the work. You read something connected with the work. And you allow all the associations connected with the work to flow. It is not yet work. But you fix a time in which the future will be reserved for work. You prepare the ground. You consecrate this time to the work. You accept the idea that a certain time must be consecrated to the work. And if a task is given you, or if you make one for yourself, you will do it during the time you have already fixed for this. The place will be made. It is by *doing* that man understands. You will see the result which this will bring you. You say you work. You think so. But no one here works yet. All this is only child's play. It is a little better than titillation. In real work, the sweat runs from the brow, it even runs from the heels.

Question: When I meet people who are slightly interested in these questions, or worried by this subject, as soon as I pass on what little experience I have, all that I have learned here diminishes and afterwards I feel smaller.

Gurdjieff: Here there is a rule; here our life is exceptional. What we say here, what we do, no one must know.

Question: But I say nothing of what we do.

Gurdjieff: But this rule also concerns the ideas. What interests you diminishes if you give it to another and you feel empty. Keep the new ideas for yourself. In life you can use the ideas as instruments. But without identifying. Everything comes out of you with your words.

Question: I think I am urged by my feeling of superiority and this is why I do it.

Gurdjieff: I will tell you something else. You have a weakness which he who works with me, must destroy. You believe. You must never believe. You must criticise everything, accept nothing which you cannot prove, like two and two make four. Believing does not count, it is worth nothing. You believe, you identify and you wish to pass on your belief with your emanations. You identify, you give all your energy. If you do not believe, if you remain quite impartial, in wishing to transmit something to someone, you do it as if you were rendering them a service. *[To someone else]* Have you experienced this?

Question: I have noticed that one loses what one has if one throws it to others.

Question: I have the impression that I cannot prevent myself from using the forces given to me by the work in order to be superior with the people whom I meet.

Gurdjieff: You are a small person. One aspect in you has grown. Six others must also grow. After this, you can imagine that you are not as others. You must not forget that the first thing to remember is your nothingness. You have a lot of imagination. If you have the knowledge of your nothingness, this idea of yourself will show you better that the others have surpassed you.

Question: When I am alone, or with substantial people, I see my nothingness. I forget it when I am with mediocre people.

Gurdjieff: I will give you a task. Work on this. Recognise your weakness and work. If you meet obstacles on the path, I will support you by correcting you.

[Mr. Gurdjieff looks at Mme V. sitting opposite and says to Mme F.]:
Now after the holidays your sister looks more like you. At first sight,
I saw that her expression had changed. I thought it was you who
was sitting over there. *[To the others]* I was sure that it was Blonde
who was over there, but it is her sister. *[To Mme V.]* Usually you are
always sitting at the side. Now you are just opposite. You are in a
good position to benefit. Now, Mr. District Attorney, if no one is
asking a question, you ask one which demands an answer easy to
formulate, an answer good for everybody. Write it and read it
afterwards.

*[While J. is writing his question, Gurdjieff asks L. to take the seat of
B. who is in the kitchen. B. comes back, sits behind Gurdjieff who asks
H. to change places with him.]*
You understand, I do not know him yet. If he asks a question and
he is not facing me, I do not see his face and I cannot make an
answer that will be subjectively good for him. It is a rule that has not
yet been formulated. Here it is: new people should sit here. For
example, he hasn't yet drunk any alcohol. Alcohol opens, it shows
many aspects of your interior; it is very important for knowing
someone. It isn't my fault, alcohol costs too much, already eighteen
hundred francs the bottle. Have you written your question, Mr.
Specialist?

J: Sir, you have enlightened me greatly on the way in which one
must accomplish one's task. To a certain degree, I'm succeeding.
But in the course of the day, one's activities are sometimes very
absorbing. One doesn't see the person who one has chosen for one's
task and afterwards one sees that the day has been empty. How can
one keep, in the absence of that person, the fire necessary for one's
task? How can one put something in its place?

Gurdjieff: In general, it is a very important thing. You have chosen
a task towards someone. But you are not always with that person.
There must be pauses. It is impossible to work all the time on an
object; you haven't enough energy. For this reason, one-half of your
time should go to your task and half for the preparation of the task.
It's a very good combination. You must use the time when you are

not seeing the person to prepare yourself. How to prepare? You can only do one thing—you can consciously increase your wish for contact with that person. You can increase it by saying to yourself: "I am." You breathe consciously. You say, "I am." When you say "I," you breathe in the air consciously with all the active elements of the air. When you say "am," you accumulate some energy in your battery and you think of using this energy. You represent to yourself the person with whom you are working and you think that when you see that person you will be more concentrated, you will have more contact with him. So that what you would have done in seven times, you will do in one. And now, doctor, explain to him in good French what I have just said.

Ab: The task is composed of two parts; in the first, you accomplish the task with the person whom you have chosen, and in the other you prepare yourself to have more direct relations with him.

Gurdjieff: No, doctor. Don't explain like that. That is not a part. There are no parts. He is absent. All his time is free. If you say "a part," it is as if you were saying, for example, one part you think, one part you do. Don't use this word. How did he ask his question? He said sometimes he was far away and he asked how he should employ his time. *All* his time for that; not a part.

[Dialogue in Russian.]

Mme de Salzmann: Mr. Gurdjieff says, why did he hook on to that?

[Silence.]

J: I have noticed—it is a verification—that, besides the fact that I am working better, in reality there are a thousand reasons that I have never seen and that appear to me now, reasons for interest in that boy. First, it facilitates my exterior work and that gives me a better relation with him; and then I do not identify with him, I do not get nervous with him.

Gurdjieff: By the way, have you noticed anything (special) since the last time I gave you a task? Has this interim been very productive?

J: Certainly yes.

Gurdjieff: But not theoretically—seriously, compact?

J: Yes.

Gurdjieff: If I say that if you work always like that, you will do in one year what you would have perhaps done in fifteen, do you believe me?

J: I can even say that I have seen it like a new door.

Gurdjieff: Brother, listen to what he says. If he continues to work well, that could help you also to continue well. Now, take as a task, helping him; and understand well that you are helping him egoistically, that you are helping him *for yourself,* so that afterwards he may help you. And for that, in order that you may remember this, I shall give you a very good means. I am going to repeat to you something that Blonde has recalled to me by association. Each day you and your brother see each other. Take as a task never to meet your brother without doing what I am going to tell you. You will say to him: "Remember yourself." And when you have said it, you will think interiorly, "I am thou, thou art I" with all your being. And you will continue this process for as long as you are able.

Al: As long as he is there?

Gurdjieff: Yes. And with these words, it is necessary that your emanations go out towards him also. Make a contact with your brother. He has the same blood as you; through the blood your brother will receive this contact. Your help can consist in that. Afterwards, if he goes out on business or for something else, from the moment he comes in, do it again. Each time you see him again after he has been absent, even if it be only for five minutes, you will begin again. If an outsider is present, you say it softly; but if he is alone, say it aloud. If someone is there, you can even make him a sign. You can press his foot, shake hands. You can have an understanding beforehand with him. You can even slap him . . . And at once you begin the task. And never forget it: that you are helping, not him, but yourself. If he can put himself solidly on his feet, he will help you afterwards. He is the only (unique) person who can help you. Doctor, have you something to say?

Ab: Sir, the preparation you were talking about a while ago, must one try to do it all the rest of the time, when one is not with the person?

Gurdjieff: That depends on the individual, how busy one is in life, what business affairs one has. You have perhaps one hundred things (to do); divide them into a hundred parts, divide your time. One part of the time you do that; another part, another thing. In principle, you should prepare yourself, but he has a task, you have

36

another. You are a doctor, you have something to do, you have many pursuits; he is only the parasite of his father, he does nothing. You, you are not a parasite. He perhaps has more of other things. But you, you have occupations. *[To J.]* If you formulate well what I have just said, there is in it a good philosophy which can serve for understanding many things. He who can grasp it will understand many things concerning education. Some other time I shall explain to you why you are, you, a parasite. Someone else, a half-parasite. Still another, a quarter-parasite. The unique parasite, do you know who he is? Our God. In the world everyone is a parasite. The only person who is not—our esteemed Mullah Nassr Eddin. He is impartial.

Ba: Who is he?

Mme de Salzmann: A wise man of the East whom you do not know as yet, who is spoken of in the book. He always has an appropriate saying for everything.

Gurdjieff: He is a wise man, unique on earth.

Mme de Salzmann: He has a maxim for every circumstance in life. For example, he says that if the father likes to dance to the tune of the violin, the son will always end by beating the (big) drum.

Gurdjieff [to Zu.]: Well, dear new person, you aren't yet seated in galoshes?

Zu: Yes, with a foot-stool.

Gurdjieff: I don't remember that he went in entirely. He is candidate for being put in galoshes. The galosh of an old Jew. Perhaps you had something to ask?

Zu: When one begins to work here (here and outside) the relations that one can have with different persons seem as before to be modified, halting. Must one keep the same expression as formerly (and one is embarrassed, for one feels oneself changed), or must one change one's face and engage oneself in a confusion and an improvement that one isn't capable of carrying out?

Gurdjieff: Well, you haven't understood the task I gave you. I told you to learn, to prepare yourself to play exteriorly a role and interiorly not to identify yourself. Interiorly, you do the work given here. Exteriorly, you change nothing, you should be as before. Before you were doing like that; now you do the same. Play a role without anyone noticing that something is going on in you. Change nothing. You remain as you were before, but you play a role. Well then, you will understand what it is to play a role. You will do the same thing you did six months ago. You change only interiorly.

Zu: You gave me that advice for one person, but it's like that in general?

Gurdjieff: For that person also it should be like that. Until you are interiorly changed, completely changed. Then at that moment, if the other notices that you have changed, he can only respect you. Otherwise, if he remembers it today that you have changed, he will take you for an idiot; he will believe that you have a new *idée fixe.* You will give him the impression of gaiety, sadness, or idiocy, or that you've fallen in love, or that you've lost at cards. People must not notice you have changed. Before them the same as before. Doctor, you have understood. He hasn't. The two things must be considered, interior and exterior.

Ab: The difficulty is that one doesn't know the person one was before. One was unconscious. One doesn't know what one was. Since one didn't see oneself. How can one imitate one's former self?

Gurdjieff: If you have an objective taste, you should know what you are. You can remember by looking backward.

Ab: But one's personality had something spontaneous which is inimitable. Perhaps in time we will manage to imitate it. But it is difficult. The imitation is wretched.

Gurdjieff: There is one thing that can help you. Each morning before going to work sit down for fifteen minutes in your bidet. *[To Denise, who is laughing]* And you, sister of charity, you understand well medical matters. Your doctor must consult you often. *[To Jacques]* Did you write it down? Also what I said about the bidet? Bravo! One word contains many explanations for him who is intelligent. One word can explain more than a thousand words. One single picture. *[To Mme Vie]* By the way, I have just noticed something. A half hour has passed; I remember that a little while ago you had the same colour as your sister. Since half an hour you have grown pale. Blonde, you have remained the same as before. Your sister has paled. It is very possible that on her right or on her left is seated a vampire who is draining her. That can be found up to fifty-four centimetres to the right or left.

Ab: I don't believe that Louise is a vampire. I'm even sure she's not.

Gurdjieff: You must never be sure. That proves that you don't know what a vampire is. Vampirism is a science. It can be practised unconsciously. Medical science does not know about it. For example, you are husband and wife. She is as thin as this, and you are like that. Three months later, he is thin like this, she is fat like that. Or the contrary. Or between brother and sister. Or two friends. Six months later everything has changed. Unconsciously. Vampirism exists consciously and unconsciously. Here where we are happens a certain vampirism. It is a very explainable law. We are all around the table. There is a chain connecting everyone. If I take the hand of my neighbour and we all hold hands, I can drain the doctor [Andrée] until she dies of it. Perhaps it is she who, not looking like a vampire, is just that. I don't know. It would be necessary to examine the question *dans l'ordre.* I see the fact. If it happens that I notice something more, I make a note of it. If twice, I remark it. If three times, it is for me a fact. Then I study seriously and specially. The first time might be an accident; I perceive it, but it is once, I say nothing. I see it a second time. So I pay attention, I look for the reason, and if it happens a third time then I study it specially. *[To Jacques]* Your work is very difficult, our esteemed chief secretary. I put myself in your place. I pity you for the time being. But I am glad for you in the future. Your bank account is growing without your having to deposit any real money.

Ba: I should like to ask a question. I should like to know . . . I remember myself many times a day, but I believe that my remembering is not voluntary. It is only the result of an association which leads me to work. How can I make a remembering that results from my wishing and not from my associations?

Gurdjieff: There exists a very good way. Is your father or your mother alive?

Ba: Both of them.

Gurdjieff: Good, you can be happy. I will give you an exercise. Learn to do it. Later I shall explain to you the details. First of all, fix a contact with your father and your mother.

Ba: When I am with them?

Gurdjieff: With or without them. You do it interiorly. For example, "I am." When they are there, you look at them. When they are not there, you represent them to yourself. You say to yourself: for each one of them. "I am thou, thou art I." You are the result of your parents. You are the same blood. Remember that. Later I will explain to you. While waiting, do this. Accustom yourself interiorly to be very quiet and to see sincerely and with affection your father, your mother. Objectively, they are more than God. God himself said: as long as your father and mother live, I do not exist for you.

Ba: Why must one thus represent to oneself one's father and mother?

Gurdjieff: You owe your life to them. But that is another question, we shall see that later. It is a law. In the meantime, take it objectively. Your father and mother are more than God. If you pray to God, God himself can send you to the devil: "after their death you will come to me" [chez moi]. It is an expression. I give you this exercise which consists of this contact in order to prepare you for another exercise. This will help you. It is difficult to remember yourself. You cannot do it theoretically, for it becomes automatic. Associations will not help you; in order to remember yourself, one must make an effort of will. You understand what I wish to say. Nothing can be born spontaneously. Your associations are not you, they are automatic. Afterwards (when you have worked) your associations will always remain automatic, but your work will have a relation, not any more with your associations, but with *you*.

[Lecture. Some books of Mr. Gurdjieff. After the dinner, Mr. Gurdjieff asks those who have returned from vacations to give him an account of their work.]

Mme Franc: I did the two exercises that you had given me during the vacation, the exercise on the division into two and on the sensations of hot, cold, and tears. I cannot say that I have had much result from these exercises, but I have had a result in the understanding. For the division into two, I cannot say that I have succeeded in doing it, but the work has given me a centre of gravity in my head. This has changed many things for me and has allowed me to de-identify myself a little from my body and I can see more clearly in my work. I know better what I am doing and how I must do it. This has changed values.

Gurdjieff: I already understood that you had a personality. Now you feel in yourself something, a separation. The body is one thing and you are another thing.

Mme Franc: That is what I feel, and it is a thing which judges.

Gurdjieff: You must congratulate yourself. I am content with all my being. It is the first thing. Without this you can never continue. Without this for ten years, a hundred years, your work shall be only titillation.

Mme Franc: It seems to me that now something has been surmounted.

Gurdjieff: Now you must fix this. One must nourish the child so that he might grow. Give him good milk, some eggs, everything that is necessary for a child. When he is a young boy, he shall be able to talk and I shall be able to understand him. For me your account is long enough.

Mme Franc: I wanted to tell you also that the exercise on the sensations had showed me that I was living in imagination, because I notice that it is only when I experience something organically that it is real; but I am not able to concentrate enough on the picture of the image.

Gurdjieff: In general this is your weakness. It is not necessary to speak of it. It is already a subjective thing. Now if I explain something, you can understand. Before you could understand nothing. The first time you took offense. And if I say the same thing now you can understand.

Mechin: I tried to continue the exercise of division into two and, seeing that I could not succeed in it, I thought that this came about because the "I" in me was not strong enough. All my attention was moved to "I am" and, in effect, this has developed little by little a very much stronger sensation, that I had never had, of "I." I have ascertained in effect that this changed all values for me, that what I had understood theoretically up till now, I understand now in a different way and this has made me understand also many problems, which fixed in me especially the necessity for me, from this moment to play a role. But as during the vacation I was rather alone in the role that I had to play, I had to play it with my parents and above all my mother; there is where the difficulty arrived. I ascertained that I was completely incapable of playing a role, that it was impossible.

Gurdjieff: You have understood what it was to play a role; you have understood what value this has for you, you have tasted it? Bravo!

Mechin: Then, I strove further with the exercise of division. I tried to understand it and one day in passing before a mirror, I was very surprised to see that I saw myself as a stranger. I thought that I ought to make use of this evidence in order to do this exercise; after, in doing the exercise I saw myself as I had seen myself in the mirror; I have had only one cold picture, without life. I saw a body without life and I tried to establish relations with my real body. In trying to do it, it seemed to me that this gave me, in advance, a taste of what might be the division. I felt that one had to do this.

Gurdjieff: It is enough, you are born. Your individuality is born. Before you were like an animal without "I." Now you have an "I" and the properties of a man. This exercise has given you these. Before you had no individuality, you were the result of your body, like a dog, a cat or a camel. Now if you have horns, you can see them and be amazed at them. Before you could see nothing. You now have an individuality which you did not have. *[Addressing the others]* He has acquired an individuality. Before he had none. He was a piece of meat. He could have worked a thousand years, he would never have had any result. You are a comrade of Mme Franc. Both of you can become initiates at the first initiation. It is a little thing but it is a big thing, a guarantee of the future. I congratulate you also. For the first time in three years I am happy internally. I am happy about my efforts. Because this is not by chance, that here are already two. You are now no longer betrothed, no longer Mechin, you are my younger brother, *[to Mme Franc]* you are my sister. We shall talk separately after.

Gurdjieff [to Yette]: You aren't happy?

Yette: Yes, and I can say that what Mme Franc has said seems to me that it was me who said it because, for some time there is something completely new in me and there is also the fear of seeing it disappear. Because in a general way, save in very rare moments, there was something in me that was not there previously and essentially something in my head, something that I felt in my head, on which I lean and which separates me from the rest, which is distinct from my body, from all that I am, from my sentiment.

Gurdjieff: You can say, perhaps, that you are one thing and your body is another thing. Before you could not say it very sincerely.

Yette: It is a thing that one can maintain?

Gurdjieff: We have thirty-three qualities of liquid that I can give you. It is not necessary to understand; you have asked me if it is possible and I have said, yes. I said also that there are thirty-three qualities of fluid.

Tracol: You have made me feel accurately, in a moment, my attitude of today towards the work. It is when you remembered during the dinner, the anecdote of the Kurde. The exercise which you gave me eighteen days ago and which consists in a continual recall: at each inhalation and at each expiration I must think "I am" and I must deposit the active elements of the air in my legs while I am reclining or seated and in the solar plexus when I am standing. I have tried to do this exercise, I try to do it always and, the more I do it, the more it becomes nearly impossible for me to do it, save in moments when I can join together the most favourable conditions. But the less I join together, the more I desire to join together and truly I could not want to abandon this exercise before having, in the end, a little better taste of what I have done. In the better moments of this exercise, not in the most favourable moments but in the moments when I work with the most intensity, that is to say in life, when I succeed in pursuing the exercise while continuing my ordinary occupations, I experience a taste which is entirely deceptive; I have the impression of living in a double dream. On the one hand I pursue my external life as in a dream and I try to play a role in it; and on the other hand, I do my work also as in a dream, and I have the impression of a role that I am going to play internally. By way of compensation, when I do this exercise only under comfortable conditions, brusquely it happens that I have a feeling of "I" which is stronger yet in the exercise of division; and I would like to recover, in my ordinary life, the taste which I had at that moment.

Gurdjieff: Continue this. You shall train yourself little by little. Make this feeling your property. One must have the feeling first. That is to say, you no longer have your associations. The feeling comes in you, it is your property but in a special state. That is to say, it cannot come in life. In a special state when you relax a little, you can remember this feeling and you must seize it.

Tracol: And, at the same time I feel that the true work is in ordinary life.

Mme de Salzmann: But one must do it before this, in a special state, and little by little you shall arrive at it in ordinary life.

Tracol: The strongest feeling of division is when I do it under comfortable conditions.

Mme de Salzmann: It is necessary for this to grow in you in these moments. After, little by little, you shall be able to make this state last.

Kahn: Several months ago I asked you this question: "When I have an impulsion of true love towards someone, it seems to me that, not only does this establish a relation between me and that person but that this gives evidence of a superior force in me." You answered me at that time that I was not to think about such things at the moment, that this was psychopathy, that I had to do my work like a service. I listened to you and I began to be able to detach myself from my body, now especially that I have seen the depth of my passivity and that I understand that I had to concentrate all my force, to put forth all my effort in opposing in myself something which "is" to my habitual nullity, now I have impulsions to become independent. For example, I have as it were an impulse to succeed in playing my true role in regard to my son or my father; I have, as it were, an impulse to succeed in becoming a man in regard to the group, but it seems to me that each of these impulsions is not yet powerful enough for the detachment to be complete. In one of my better moments of work, I saw recently all my body, all my emotions, all my sentiment and my usual desires as that which I had to succeed in killing in me in order to attain birth, and I understood that I would succeed in being what I want to be if I succeeded in making that which I am die. Thus, I ask you now, I ask myself and I ask you also, if I could not be aided in my efforts by a relationship of what there is of an "I" in me with a superior form—if this is not the impulsion that is lacking in me?

Gurdjieff: No, continue. Why do you use the word "true"? You cannot yet have a "true love." One aspect of "true love" must be to hate justly, to hate objectively, not the object but its manifestations. You cannot yet use the word "true." While waiting, continue to amass material. But cease saying the word "true." One must not give this value to things. You cannot yet love, you can do nothing. You do not yet have the feeling and I have need of you having it. When you shall be able to have an impulsion, I shall be able to give you satisfaction. How to use it, how to direct it, how to realise it. I see that the form of work which I have given you has helped you; and if this has helped you, it is not necessary to change.

Kahn: This work has brought me what nothing else has.

Gurdjieff: The rest is worth nothing. Although to that which might be to us, there is not yet enough of it in you for a "true impulsion."

Gurdjieff [to Simone]: You understood? For you also something is opened?

Simone: Indeed, while listening to Mechin, Gabrielle and Yette speak, I was with them.

Gurdjieff: You felt with your head, with your intelligence. For example, for Mechin, long before him you had understood; he understands less than you, but he understands with his whole being. He understood with his individuality, you with your body. For me, this has more value than yours.

Simone: I feel something in my head now that stays nearly all the time; it is not very strong but it is almost constant, something that makes me see beings and things in a different way.

Gurdjieff: This is normal. Little by little everything must be different. You are beginning to have a true view. You had, up to the present, a fantastic point of view.

S: I do not succeed in having emotion when I concentrate. I can make my head free, but I do not succeed in feeling a strong emotion. I have the impression of running up against a barrier and not being able to go further.

Gurdjieff: You fall down right at the beginning because of one small thing. With the head no one ever can have emotion. The head is one thing. Emotion is another thing. Emotion is a function of the body. With the head one can only constate, one cannot feel. I am sitting. I have a pain. Here I am hot, here I am cold. I observe this with my head and I feel it with my solar plexus. I feel that here I am hot and there cold. And I constate it with my head. If I concentrate specially, I can constate it. But I become identified if I think I can do more than that. I constate that I am here like this, there like that, as a whole I am like that. You never notice anything with your head. Your head is capable of constating only if you put attention on something. It is only with special attention that the head can constate. The head is like an apparatus, it plays the role of police. But the centre of gravity of your presence is in your solar plexus, which is the centre of feeling. That is where things happen. The head is like a typewriter. You understand what I say? Your question proves that you do not work as I have just been saying; it is necessary to find the way to work like that. Not with your head. Your head can only constate, not in any way work. You must work with your sensation and your feeling. As for the head, it can see whether they are together or separate. The head is not a part of the organism, it is separate from the organism. The body can die, the head also. But the head can die and the rest go on living. The head is nothing, a function, a typewriter, an apparatus. When you concentrate your attention in your head, you can constate what goes on in you. But the head is nothing, it is a stranger to the organism. She [the one who asked the question] wants to feel with her head. Never will she be able to. The head is alien to the body. The head can play the role of police, but only of police, who looks how everything goes on, like a watchman. It watches how the functions of your presence are working. Do you understand me?

S: Yes.

Gurdjieff: You understand the reasons for our being in our situation and what you have to do?

S: Could you show me a task? I have tried several, but none of them suits me and I do not know which one to choose.

Gurdjieff: Look. I take up an unusual posture, a posture which is difficult for my body because I am not used to it. In myself, my functions are working and my two centres—feeling and sensation. I sense the awkwardness of my posture and I feel the awkwardness of it. For I am not accustomed to it. With my head I look to see what it is. I study. Ah, yes! It is like that. And here, it is like that. That is the way you do this. It is a simple thing. You keep the three centres separate in you. You understand this very simple thing. It is an unpleasant posture. I may fall. I look: I sense this: I feel that. Ah! Yes—it is like that. I observe. With my head, I collect material. I compare. With my head, with my logic, I find the reasons: why, how. On the one hand, I sense, on another, I feel. And in this way, do you see, the three centres are occupied with this work. You separate your three centres. I advise you to do this in the meanwhile. When you have come to know your centres, then we will take another exercise. I advise you to take this posture as an example. You can take another one—any other uncomfortable posture. It is a very simple thing and a very good one. Among others, T., it is a very good exercise for you too. Up to now, you have not yet separated your three centres. In many things you have gone further, but as far as this very simple thing is concerned, you are an outsider. Every man must recognise in himself three qualities of sensation. In each person there are three centres, three directors. And these three directors can give a fourth one, who can be the "I."

[Noise of breakage in the kitchen. Mr. Gurdjieff speaks in Russian to Mme de Salzmann.]

I am saying to Mme de Salzmann, that she has never yet constated what I have just been saying to her. She had not understood until now. Now she has understood how much my institute used to cost every month and why I had to pay every month three or four million francs. One aspect, amongst others: how many things there were spoilt, broken, messed up.

[Mme de Salzmann gives as an example the gardening tools.]

48

There, it was an institute. It was for the Work. It was to be expected. Here, it is not an institute. Here, it is necessary to help me, and every day people break things of mine. And it is I who have to pay. There, it was one thing: people were learning. A learner does break things. Here it is another thing. Each one must take care of everything. But each week, what I have diminishes by ten or twenty pieces. The year has how many weeks? And the war has lasted four years. Can you imagine? If you count how much stuff I have lost? But people don't understand this.

[Dialogue in Russian with Mme de Salzmann.]

You are lucky. You are lucky enough to have a short memory. What has just fallen back there, I shall remember for three hours. What a lot it costs me! It has the effect on me of an earthquake.

[Mme de Salzmann jokes with T. about Turkish baths.]

B: I would like to ask a question about concentration. When I want to collect myself and I fix my attention on a point, my thinking seems empty. Instead of being concentrated, it is empty. It is still, but it is empty and this stillness does not exclude associations. On the other hand, when I am held by an external object, my thought is not still but it seems to me much more concentrated, I have no associations. My thought is never fixed but it seems to me far more concentrated than when my concentration is intentional; the stilling of thought I arrive at seems to me the opposite of true concentration.

[While Mme de Salzmann is translating, B. explains his question to A.]

Gurdjieff [to A.]: What he is telling you interests me very much. How do you explain the question?

A: When B. tries to concentrate, his thought agglutinates.

Gurdjieff: No. Don't say it like that. I am going to give an explanation which will be very good for you too and which will help you very much. I can say it now. Try to understand. To begin with, the secret is "I am." You begin like that. Now, I feel "I." But how do I feel "I"? What is "I"? I feel this place (the top of the arm) and this one (solar plexus). Try that now. And at the same time, I constate with my head. Do that. It will make you understand. I feel and sense these two parts (the top of the arm and the solar plexus) and at the same time, with my head, I constate what is going on. Do that now.

If you do it, you will understand what has been missing in you up till now. It is very simple. Afterwards, when you have felt that with one part of your attention and with your head, you will be able to travel in yourself, freely. Associations, that is another thing. Leave them alone; they are "cheap" things—little things. I am bigger than my associations. He who has constated something new, let him say it. Something misunderstood, or perhaps you have constated something good for you.

[S. makes a sign meaning no.]

Has anyone discovered an America? T.?

T: No, not yet.

Gurdjieff: Blonde, and you?

Mme F: That real concentration comes only with sensing.

Gurdjieff [to A.]: Have you understood?

A: Sensing, yes, but I do not understand the feeling of the body.

Gurdjieff: The whole time, you feel this *[shows the top of the arm and solar plexus]* and you observe with your head. You do these three things all the time.

A: I find this increases the sensation of presence.

Gurdjieff: Thanks to this exercise, you will increase your force of concentration. It is made for that. Now explain to him [to B.] that he must do this exercise. Through this, he will be able to arrive at sensing. He is not able to today. This exercise will help him.

[J. begins to read the question he has written]: More and more I feel how much my work is mental, how little it animates me. And I have understood that I truly cannot approach my work with real fire [élan].

Gurdjieff: Excuse me, but what you have just said is not logical. One destroys the other. I don't understand what you wish to say. Don't read, put your paper away.

J: I lack an impulse for my work. I don't succeed in approaching my work in a satisfactory manner unless I feel a certain urge which can only come to me from a clear realisation of my present situation and my present nothingness. I have understood that very clearly. And that made me understand that I ought to have remorse of conscience for this nothingness. But I can't go further than this statement. What can I do to have remorse of conscience?

Gurdjieff: That question carries with it seven aspects; not one, but seven. One I will tell: Every man when he comes into the world, comes here for certain reasons. There are causes, that is to say, outside forces have created him. These forces perhaps were not obliged to give you life. Are you glad to be alive? Is life worth something to you? Well then, if you are alive and glad of it, you should pay something in return. For example, I see your mother here. But for her, you would never have come into the world. It is to her that you owe your life. If you are glad to live, you must repay her. You are of age now, the time has come to settle your debts. One of the chief causes of your being alive is your mother. It is because of her that you have your pleasures and that you have possibilities of developing yourself. One of the reasons, one of the aspects of your coming into this world is your mother. And I ask you, have you begun to pay your debts to her?

J: No.

Gurdjieff: There are still six other aspects. But I speak to you of one aspect. Begin, then, by this first aspect: your mother. Repay her. Even if she is objectively bad, she is your mother. And how can you pay her? You should unify her life. But instead of that, what do you do? You make her life more difficult. You unnerve her, you irritate her. Unconsciously, remorse of conscience could flow from that. Take the year that has just passed, remember: often you have been very bad. You are *merde*. You have not fulfilled your obligations. If you have understood this, remorse can begin in you. This is but one aspect. I could explain to you six others, but forget them. Before knowing them, begin by this one. For the past two years, how many times have you been bad, very bad, to her? Remember this and try to repair the past with your future in the present. It is a very difficult thing. If you forget, if you do not do it, it is your fault and doubly your fault; first you are to blame for the past; and you are a second time to blame for not repairing it today. A good answer, is it not? Everyone here is glad. Except one person—do you know who? Your mother. Madame, it is for the benefit of your son that I say this.

[He speaks in Russian with Mme de Salzmann.]

Mme de Salzmann [to Mme E.]: You might think that if Mr. Gurdjieff speaks like this, it is because he is our kind host and because you are here. But it isn't for that.

Jac: I've thought about what you said to me the other day, that I must choose: "All or nothing." I've decided to take a task and stick to it no matter what happens. This task was to put aside a certain time of the day to do an exercise, the exercise of the extended arms. And in trying to do this exercise, I've understood truly for the first time what it is to be a nonentity. Until now, I thought I had understood, but it was for exterior reasons only. I saw that I was incapable of doing anything whatever, because something in me refused to make an effort.

Gurdjieff [first speaks in Russian to Mme de Salzmann]: Excuse me. Perhaps you believed I had forgotten you. I asked Mme de Salzmann: "When everyone went away for the holidays, I gave to each one a bottle of medicine to take while working. Is it possible that I did not give it to you?" She tells me that I did not give it to you. Now I understand why you asked me that question. If you had had that bottle you wouldn't have thought that way about your nothingness. *[He speaks to all]* He felt in general a nothingness. But today he possesses nothing; he has accumulated nothing during his holidays. You on the contrary are little by little reaping the results of your work. Now you have a basis for measuring how that can be done. *[To Ab.]* Do you understand now the force of chemistry?

Ab: I took about a third of it.

Gurdjieff: That is *your* business. You've had only a third of the force. That is not my fault; if you take all, you will have three times more force. It is for that that I said it. Perhaps you didn't give enough value to this medicine. Perhaps that will give you a remorse of conscience in the future in order to obtain another quality of attention. As to him [Lac.] I can say I regret not having given him the bottle I gave to everyone for the holidays. Mme de Salzmann says I did not give one to him. I understand the reason for his question. If he had had his bottle he would have done something else with his time during the holidays—he would not have asked that question. You understand, Tracol? I'm sorry he is not in the Saturday group. He isn't and it's for that reason he asked the question. If he has asked that idiotic question it's because he hadn't had his bottle of medicine. It is your fault, it's the fault of Madame the Présidente and the fault of all his friends. He's been here a long time; he's been your friend a long time; and for a long time he's been deprived. It's the fault of Mme de Salzmann, of the Présidente, of every person here.

[He offers cigarettes to Mme Et.]

Mother, you deserve to have everything. You should have everything. Your sons should give you everything, and the friends of your sons. You have brought up your sons to a responsible age. They should give you what you care for. If you like cigarettes, you should have cigarettes. If you haven't any, it is the fault of your two results; they must be annihilated.

Lac: May I finish my question?

Gurdjieff: Finish.

Lac: I have noticed in doing this exercise that for the first time and for a very short moment, I had the feeling of being free, free of this inertia against which I am always struggling, and that has given me the exact taste of what could be liberty.

[Mme de Salzmann translates, but Gurdjieff stops her.]

Gurdjieff: I've already understood. It's the same reason. You have understood with your head, but your organism has not the possibility of being what your head wishes. Well then, the chemical matters I spoke of can give you that and accumulate results in you and give you the fire for revitalising your functions. It's the same reason.

Whose fault it is I do not know, but for the future you should take every measure—ask, beg, supplicate Mme de Salzmann to help you. Mme President also has the possibility of getting you into the Saturday group. *[To Mme Er.]* You ought to see to it that your title has a meaning. In the beginning you thought it was a joke, but it's taken a serious turn. Tracol, how is your pupil [Gerb]? You ought to help your pupil, enlighten him so that he may understand. He has a very sympathetic exterior. I know him exteriorly but not interiorly. For that, he must manifest with his tongue. You should help him so I may understand his interior. In the same way that the Prosecuting Attorney is governor for her [Mlle Dol.]. You have noticed that when I know someone well, I am able to give good advice? Now, I cannot. I must know with what he is stuffed. As for her [Mlle Dol.], I know with what spices she is stuffed.

[He Jokes with Mlle Dol. and Sunn about saving cigarettes, invites certain people for Sunday, gives bonbons and dismisses them.]

[Being present: Mme de Salzmann, Miss Gordon, Mlle Abadi, Mlle Regnault, Mme Franc, Mlle Leprudhomme, Mme Tracol, Nano, Mechin, Lebeau, Dr. Aboulker, Luc Dietrich, Jacques and Alfred. Dinner after the reading.]

Gurdjieff: Young man, I noticed you a little while ago and then you disappeared. I am very interested to know how you passed your holidays and what you have brought back for my disillusions and— the contrary of disillusions.

[A discussion here about this word.]

Well, young man, I'm very interested to hear your report. Everyone who has returned has made his report; I know them now more or less. In order that I know you better in the future, for your future relations, I wish to know how you passed your time and at the same time perhaps my answer to you will be useful for somebody else. So, if you do not wish to make that somebody happy, you can refuse and you and I can speak alone together. But if you decide that your report can be useful, make it.

Lebeau: Over the holidays my work consisted in playing all kinds of roles. I have the impression that I am a little freer with respect to other people from myself and from the results of my actions. In the four days since I returned to Paris, I feel in me a kind of vague fear of a defence reaction. It seems to me that everything that is around me is made to eat me up, that I am more dependent on exterior things, of success or failure, as if a new force wanted to destroy something in me. And I would almost say that this terrifies me, because it seems to me to be something essential and I should like to know what I can do to struggle against it.

Gurdjieff: Do you wish to have first an explanation for that and go on afterwards or do you wish to continue now?

Lebeau: I wish to say something else. Several months ago you advised me to try to be a good egoist. Now in regard to others, I feel many attitudes in me that seem to me to be the result of what I did in the holidays. There is the old thing: Give, have pity, that is always there in one sense. There is a new thing that causes me to consider others as means or instruments and that I can say to myself let them all fall dead, what difference does it make to me. There is a third attitude which consists of running away from them. Sometimes it's one, sometimes the other, sometimes all three together. I don't manage to conciliate them and that gives me a bizarre feeling. And what I say about others I would be able to say a little in the same way about myself. To consider myself as an instrument. With the same actions in respect to others. That produces a certain feeling of uneasiness that I cannot harmonise.

[A rather long silence.]

That's all I had to say.

Gurdjieff: There are three questions and you understand that you should have from me three explanations. First, there where you were during a special period you created for yourself life habits very different from the usual ones, quite other conditions, another tempo for your functions: an absolutely different quality. And you come back here. Here is another situation, other conditions which you experienced, as you related. And now if you continue to be afraid, then the same thing will happen to you that happens to a monk in a monastery. In a monastery he works very well all alone. But in life he goes in quite another direction as soon as he has relations with others. What you have gained while away you must use—fix it in your life. Begin a very difficult task. Do not identify. Fix everything that you have acquired. If you do not make efforts to fix it in yourself, exactly what happens to the monks will happen to you. All will be lost.

Lebeau: That's a little like what I felt: the need to fix all that.

Gurdjieff: It will be a very hard time of attention. Not to identify oneself and continue to play the new role here. Outwardly to act the same as you used to, and inwardly to hold your state and fix it firmly in the conditions of your present life. Thus you will have the profit of everything that you did during your holidays. If not, all will become a hodgepodge. Here are my instructions. Have no mercy on yourself, don't spare yourself and, pitilessly, crystallise in yourself even in the new conditions of life, the impressions and associations of the summer.

Lebeau: What makes the work more difficult is that during the holidays I had each time an exact role to play; here I must find something else.

Gurdjieff: That is the reason it is difficult and I told you to make an effort. You must play your old role and let your interior state be the new condition that you have acquired. Next you asked a second question about egoism. About that I have said in general that he who wishes to be a real altruist in the future should be in the present an absolute egoist. But this summer you thought that meant including your near ones—your father and mother. But with them you cannot be an egoist, you cannot act that way. With them, nature does not permit it. With others you can. From that comes the misunderstanding; I did not specify the object of the exercise and you took your father and mother. But that depends on the object. When I spoke I did not speak of the father and mother, I spoke in general. You should outwardly play a role and inwardly not identify. And you did this with your mother. I said you should be a pure egoist in order to have the possibility to be a real future altruist. But you could not be a real egoist with your father and mother this summer. That is the reason it was difficult. You took them as the objects of the exercise, but you could not do it, for it was against nature.

Lebeau: That is correct. But even in respect to others, pity came in. When I was playing my role, there was pity. Not especially for each one but for the total of everything together that was there like that.

Gurdjieff: Then it was always when you were coming to see your father and mother and that continued automatically by the given impulse. You were not at peace after you had seen them, but you didn't have to have pity. You ought to be selfish. The others didn't exist for you; in the future you will be standing on your own feet. But at present you haven't pity; it is your task. It is different when you come to meet your father and mother, pity comes automatically and even remorse of conscience. You have confused things. I didn't warn you when I explained egoism and I didn't say anything special about this where parents are concerned. And now the third question: I shall give you a task and if you wish, all your future even, will depend on the way in which you pass your time in the months to come. On this depends all your future. This summer you acquired a good material; fix it in you for life. It is very hard work. Remember yourself. All the time. Fix it with "I am." Constantly in life try,

57

continue, completely egoistically. No pity. Don't help anyone and have a clear conscience. When you grow strong you will see a hundred times more. Now you are not strong, you cannot do anything. Forget everything for the sake of your future. And your future depends on continuing the egoism exercise. So continue this. How can you manage not to forget? "I am, I can be, I can be that." Not to be egoist in the future. Try. Remember yourself as often as possible. "I am." Have the sensing of yourself as often as possible and the more you are able to remember yourself inwardly, the better will your future be.

Lebeau: Sometimes I almost wanted not to allow my egoism to be free, because I was surprised to feel it within myself like a hungry animal and I was rather afraid of it.

Gurdjieff: You went away in order to nourish yourself and rest. You prepared material so that you could work. So even if you had acted like a vampire it would have been excusable. You had to have nourishment. By the way, I have constated that the majority of those who have returned from the holidays are off balance. This is normal just as the time before going away was normal. Everyone has forgotten that man does not consist of one person but of two or three persons. They forgot this while away. They acted as if they were one person. But they are not one person. They have developed one part and forgotten the others and today they feel a disharmony in themselves. One, for example, has developed his body very well and has neglected his individuality. And everyone feels a disharmony. They are not just one person but three different persons. All three must be developed. For each one of the three, time and measures must be taken. If, for example, someone has developed his mind well and not his body, he is more of a nonentity than before. If you wish to formulate that, it could be done like this: He has three persons in him; one is eight years old, another is forty, the other a hundred and five. Picture that to yourself. Three persons like that live in one room. They can have nothing in common with each other either of agreement or any work in common. The person who is sixty cannot act like a child of eight and the child of eight cannot understand what the person of sixty can.

Do not forget that man is made of three persons. For each of the three there must be a different exercise. All three must work, and not just one, only one, just from one side. That would be lopsided. All three must advance together. He who during the holidays developed his feeling centre and if it does not correspond well with his body, will not be able to make progress. He will have to decrystallise and destroy the work he has done while away in order to be able to develop the second part. The holidays have been very good for one thing. They gave you a taste for understanding what you ought to understand. Another year is beginning for the work. Use your mistakes and your observations to work now seriously and to have good results.

But you can use what you gained during the holidays if you repair [make up for] what you did not do: put aside what you developed, put your attention and work on the side that wasn't developed. When the two are harmonised, they will be united. He who develops himself only with his mind is nothing; if only with the body, he also is nothing. Both are needed. Now you possess already the material which will give you a good chance of succeeding at a more useful and greatly profitable task.

You [Lebeau] begin again with another kind of attention and another understanding. Your work must consist of two things: Get better acquainted with your nonentityness and remember yourself often, as often as possible, with the sensing of remembering yourself: "I am," and of experiencing yourself. And each time that that reverberates in your common presence you remember that you are. And all the impressions, all the associations of your holidays, make them reverberate in your common presence and remember that you are. And when you remember that, say "I am" and feel in all your being that you are. Mr. Attorney, have you understood what I said? As an exercise, can you repeat what I said, or at least the last part?

Jacques: I've been too busy writing to be able to repeat it like that now.

Gurdjieff: Well, let's make a compromise. It will be your brother who will speak. Brother, are you there? Will you repeat?

[Alfred tries.]

You can't repeat anything. That proves that what goes in one ear goes out of the other. Now you are seated in galoshes. Really there is only one person here who can help us. It is our professional writer, my colleague.

[Luc speaks from his text.]

Write, Mr. Attorney. What he says interests me very much. It is very light. What I said was heavy. Thank you, little one. But have you finished? Please go on.

Luc: It's what I understood the best.

Gurdjieff: Don't you want to render it still more comprehensible? I said another thing about remembering yourself. Miss Understanding, you have perhaps something to say which will make heavier what he has said?

Simone: You said that we should use the material we accumulated in the holidays and that everything that arose in us which was an occasion for self-remembering we should use for a more intense self-remembering in all our common presences for crystallising the results of our holidays.

Gurdjieff: Why do you use my words? Crystallise is my own word. Find another word.

Mme de Salzmann: To cover, clothe, condense, fix.

Gurdjieff: Yes, clothe. Why didn't you say that? Go on, go on, that was only a remark.

[Simone is silent.]

Well, if she cannot go on, Mr. Attorney, I advise you to put on your amiable expression and request the doctor to repeat what I have said.

[Jacques asks her—Mlle Dr. Abadi.]

Mlle A: You said one must remember oneself with all ones presence and that one must profit from all ones mistakes and use all ones mistakes and everything that one has noted to make of them factors for self-remembering. I didn't notice anything else.

Luc: I thought I understood you to tell us to profit from all the times when we are most aroused, even taken by anger and negative emotions, to profit from this current of force which runs through us; to use it. Profit from everything which raises our temperature.

Gurdjieff: That also. I have also said that. Has anyone anything else to say?

Kahn: You have many times spoken of seven aspects, of the different aspects of one question. For a long time I didn't understand. Afterwards I understood better, I saw that you were seeing many aspects in me which were mixed up for me but which you were distinguishing and I wanted to ask you if we also were able to distinguish different aspects.

Gurdjieff: Please do not say "we." Say "I," when you speak of yourself, and not "we." If you do not know your own aspects, how can you note the aspects of another person? Ask me something practical. The other is only curiosity.

Kahn: No, it isn't from curiosity.

Gurdjieff: Then formulate it differently. There are three aspects that you are able to see in different friends of yours—where is to be found their centre of gravity, their individuality. Of your three friends, one has his centre of gravity in his mind; another is like a cow with centre of gravity in his body; the third is like an hysterical woman, he manipulates for everything. There are three aspects of individuality. Study that, it's a good soil. *[To Aboulker]* What are you laughing at?

Aboulker: The hysterical woman.

Gurdjieff: There isn't a better illustration for the emotional centre than the hysterical woman. She feels everything, even what doesn't exist.

Kahn: You have made me feel that I have many aspects without my being able to know them or even distinguish them from the others.

Gurdjieff: By your work, you should succeed in distinguishing them. Separate them. You have seven aspects of density. At times I am very heavy, at times very light. Learn to tell them apart. When you see someone, you will see what aspect he has. Another time we will be able to talk about the fundamental aspects. First recognise the others, it is useless to talk about the rest before. The theory should go with the practice.

Lacaze: Mr. G. . . .

Gurdjieff: Father! Tell me what goes on with your better half. I haven't seen her for a long time. Perhaps she is preparing a little new result for you?

Lacaze: No, no. Mr. Gurdjieff, there is something in me that opposes my work and helps my inertia. In general I recognise the fact that mere life can't give me anything; and yet there is something in me that waits for life, not only something exterior but something interior, that says it would be preferable to have a change of exterior conditions which would give me everything I love in general. And even when I am sure intellectually that only work is important for me and that I should put everything on the work, I feel something in me that is convinced of the contrary and which tries to go in this direction.

Gurdjieff: What direction?

Lacaze: Away from the work.

Gurdjieff: You do not know this direction?

Lacaze: It's the opposite direction from the work.

Gurdjieff: I see one small thing. If you win the five million in the National Lottery, all that will disappear. It's too bad that it doesn't depend on me. Now ask me exactly what you want from me.

Lacaze: I want to know what I can do about this. Isn't there something that should be satisfied? Something just? Or would that be only a justification of inertia?

Gurdjieff: What you lack is remorse of conscience. You do not think of that. Have you children?

Lacaze: Yes.

Gurdjieff: How many?

Lacaze: Three.

Gurdjieff: Three! Well, if you have three children you should know that your life doesn't exist any more for you yourself, but for your children. Is it for your children that you do everything or for your own satisfaction? Ask yourself that. If you have asked yourself that, I can tell you that you have no remorse of conscience towards your children. That can serve you as a reminding factor to make you work in order for you to become a real man. You have no right to your own satisfactions, that is finished. Everything is for your children— everything that you have for possibilities. It is an objective necessity. But you do not think of it, you continue to act the egoist. Your question proves it. So have remorse of conscience for the future. Repair the past for the sake of the future. You are obliged to work for your children. This idea held in you can play the role of a factor, at times for remembering yourself, at times for giving you strength for the future. And with it you will be able to repair the past. You do not like this truth. But I tell it as an example. There are a thousand other things, this is an example. But you can find something else to furnish you with a material capable of making you find remorse of conscience. Only this remorse can crystallise the factors which will serve you in remembering yourself. The rest cannot. Only remorse of conscience can. It is here that you talk; and afterwards in life you forget everything. In life you have six days, twenty-three hours and fifty minutes. Here, ten minutes. What you do and gain here during ten minutes, you lose in life. Never is there a reminding factor, only remorse can give it to you.

Solange: I should like to be able to overcome a fear that I had as a child and which has returned. Sometimes at night I have a sort of apprehension, an anguish that seizes me in the back at the spinal column. I can do nothing against it. I had it as a child of twelve or thirteen, because I used to read detective stories and things like that. Afterwards I didn't have it any more and now it's come back worse than ever.

Gurdjieff: That's a medical matter. I can't say much about that. In the meantime before going to sleep give yourself an alcohol rub—or with just cold water or cologne. Then I will arrange an interview with you and some doctor and myself and we can talk seriously about curing you.

Solange: But I am already doing that; you advised me to three weeks ago and I'm using cold water.

Gurdjieff: Then do it more, the water has prepared the pores and now you must rub yourself with alcohol. If you haven't any, I'll give you a small bottle.

[Present: Mme de Salzmann, André Abadi, G. Franc, Louise Leprudhomme, Miss Gordon, Yette, Simone, Nano, R. Daumal, Philippe, Méchin, Tracol, Aboulker, Kahn, Luc, Lebeau, J. and A. Etiévant, J. Crochereau. After the reading of Pogossian, Mr. Gurdjieff asked if anyone had made any observations concerning the separation exercise.]

Aboulker: I continued with this exercise, and although I have not achieved everything, I have succeeded a little this summer, during the holidays. Now I find much less than I did back then. Yesterday I tried it with more energy than is usual. I felt a quite considerable warmth, but I have not been able to reach a point of coming out of myself. I spoke with Mr. Gurdjieff at the beginning of September. He told me that he would give me an exercise to help me regain the taste of division which I had experienced. I would request Mr. Gurdjieff to now give me this exercise.

Gurdjieff: I am going to give a little exercise. A very easy one. For example, when you're sitting in your armchair, get up and sit back down again alternatively. Do it interiorly. Externally, you remain seated as normal, while you do this exercise innerly. Move interiorly only.

Aboulker: Must I have an interior sensation?

Gurdjieff: Yes. You will even be able to do this exercise on the train or on the metro. But no one must be able to see anything exteriorly. You can do it from different sitting postures, but not while standing. One thing is requisite: it must always be possible to physically perform it. That is, you must be in a position where you could easily do it. If you're lying down you won't be able to do it.

Luc: I have observed that I can separate out from myself very strongly when I make a very brief effort. But the effort is lost and disappears when I try to keep it.

Gurdjieff: It is not necessary to do it strongly. You could acquire a fixed idea about it. It is never necessary to force oneself: what is necessary is to do it gradually.

Luc: I have expressed myself rather badly. It isn't the efforts I make to succeed which are strong, it's in the impression that I

64

receive the strength, so long as the effort is brief.

Gurdjieff: It's in the effort. All that you do without using the automatism is an effort. When you do everything automatically, to act a little more consciously will be an effort. But it isn't necessary for you to do anything vehemently.

Luc: I focus all my forces for a very short period, as if trying to overcome some obstacle.

Gurdjieff: It is not necessary to do that. Do your exercise just as a service, and little by little, you will arrive there. I did say, on one occasion, that it was better to work intensely and for short moments. But the intensity is in the attention, the intensity of concentration, and not in any shock.

Luc: It is concentrated, because the wrenching of myself is almost sad.

Gurdjieff: Your effort must be to concentrate, not to wrench.

Luc: But my nature refuses to separate itself out.

Mme de Salzmann: If you concentrate in yourself more, it will happen by itself.

Gurdjieff: Tense yourself organically or you will also tense your feeling. Here is an exercise. Tense the base of your foot. Do it with your three centres. Do this exercise, then stop, and then begin it again. Do not do it with one centre alone. Do it well, with three centres. It is an independent exercise, for you. First do that, and then try your big exercise. Tell me in a week what result you've obtained and I will advise you further.

Louise: I am no longer doing the separation exercise. I am involved now in concentrating myself in my head, to see my body. I then sense my body as lighter and full of light, only I have the impression that I sense myself, that I see myself, and that it is not my head. I have the impression that I see myself as more than my head, more than my body.

Gurdjieff: But separation is exactly that.

Louise: I could not, however, feel myself as double.

Gurdjieff: But you can't feel yourself at all. Your double is incorporeal, you are not able to feel it. It is something which is beyond bodily. You will sense it later, when it has been coated with a body. I am going to do something exceptional for you. Mme de Salzmann will teach you the first of the Sunday group exercises. You don't belong in that group, but you can do their first exercise. I have already explained this subject to everyone. But I will explain it again to Mme de Salzmann and to the doctor. *[To André]* You will be able to help Mme de Salzmann to explain to Louise what you understand better than she does.

Lebeau: Several times now, I have arrived at a feeling of vibrations of some sort which bathe my whole body when I prepare myself to do the separation exercise.

Gurdjieff: When you prepare yourself? But does that happen when you are in the midst of the exercise?

Lebeau: No, not exactly. At the time, these vibrations give me the impression of dissolving and numbing my body. I have the impression at that very moment of two separated things. But when I try to concentrate these vibrations, I can arrive at nothing.

Gurdjieff: Exactly the same. Now take all steps to try and enter into the Sunday group. Do what you must to merit entry. For you also, the first exercise is necessary. Without that you could work for a thousand years and all you would receive is fixed ideas and end up a candidate to enter into a madhouse. While waiting (to join the Sunday group), do the exercise solely as a service. But arrange to speak with Mme de Salzmann either tomorrow or the day after and she will explain to you.

[Then Mr. Gurdjieff said to R. Daumal that he had spoken especially of him to Mme de Salzmann and she would explain.]

[After lunch.]

Philippe: I would like to ask you a question I had asked four weeks ago, when you told me not to continue the exercises. But I would like to begin them again them now.

Gurdjieff: Well tell me how you've spent your time.

Philippe: I have been able to rest myself, not a lot, but a little.

Gurdjieff: What do you mean by "not a lot"? Have you written anything?

Philippe: I have.

Gurdjieff: Well, if you have been writing then how can you have been resting?

Philippe: I haven't been able to do anything else, I have to earn my living.

Gurdjieff: Then what you have written, you've sold, and you've received some money. How have you been able to rest while working? Perhaps you need a special physical respite. How do you work on yourself when you wish to rest yourself?

Philippe: Over there, I was able to sleep, to sleep well. I didn't do the exercises: you had told me to stop. I haven't worked, and without the work, I haven't relaxed either.

Gurdjieff: If you cannot sleep here, but you have slept there, we have a sign of work. You have arranged your life a little less mechanically. If it wasn't automatic, then you were working.

Philippe: I was able to sleep.

Gurdjieff: You slept a good deal? Have you put on weight?

Philippe: I haven't weighed myself.

Gurdjieff: But you wish now to work consciously?

Philippe: I feel the need for an inflexible rule. I would like to introduce into my life a very firm rule. I sense that I would be able to maintain it. I have never sensed my slavery so much as now. I have, without doubt, had that knowledge, but never have I sensed it to this degree.

Gurdjieff: Do this exercise as your work. Two, three times each day, when lying down, relax yourself. Your thoughts, your feeling, all your functions must be occupied with that. Your small muscles, you middling muscles, your large muscles must be relaxed.

Make a programme. Decide how much time you will spend on it. Fifteen minutes, half an hour, one hour. Arrange to do it three times each day. Do it as a service.

I repeat again: large muscles, middling muscles, small muscles. You don't know your small muscles. You will get to know them when you start relaxing yourself. You will learn that you have three qualities of muscles, and these three qualities of muscles must become passive, without activity, completely tranquil, without action or manifestation.

Make a programme beforehand, decide how many times. The first time, perhaps, it will be mediocre, you won't receive anything. The second time it will be better, and by the tenth time, perhaps, you will have the taste of mediocre relaxation but also of good relaxation.

You have these three qualities of muscles in your finger as much as in your head.

67

Lie down, and make your individuality like a warden in control. If your muscles do not relax, then smack that spot. At the beginning, do it lying down, but when you have the taste you can do it sitting or even standing. Indeed, you can do it even while walking. For example, if you walk to the Champs-Elysées, you cannot relax your legs, you will know that at the very first reverberation. But relax your right side or your left side or your navel. Do you understand?

Philippe: Very well.

Gurdjieff: Then have you understood that I am giving you good advice? What do you think? Doctor Aboulker has been doing the washing up, he hasn't been able to hear the exercise which I have given you, so beyond doubt, this will be good advice for him too. You can repeat it to him: it will be useful for your subjective comprehension as well as for him.

Philippe [to Dr. Aboulker]: I said to Mr. Gurdjieff that I had never sensed myself as such a slave as I do now. I need an inflexible rule which I will impose on myself every day. Mr. Gurdjieff has advised me to decontract myself entirely three times a day—the large, the medium and the small muscles, and to do it lying down at the start. It is possible to do it sitting, or even standing, but, for the moment, it is necessary to do it lying down during the time dedicated to it. It is necessary, at first to decontract the big muscles, then the medium which can decontract the big muscles, then the medium ones which can decontract themselves only when the big ones are decontracted, then the small ones. While one is walking it isn't possible to decontract the leg muscles, but one can decontract another part of the body. And during this time to do nothing, to decontract even the smallest tensions. *[To Mr. Gurdjieff]* These muscles are the ones of which you spoke to the doctor when you gave him the exercise of not moving.

Gurdjieff: I can say nothing now, but you will understand when you've done that. You already know that you have three categories of muscles, but when you do your exercise you will understand this.

Philippe: Sometimes movements start up in us. For example, a gesture is born in anger: I clench my fist, the hand remains inert, but the muscle tenses itself.

Gurdjieff: More: when you think of a certain person, your muscles move in the direction of the person thought of. What you need is to relax and to occupy your thought with this exercise.

Aboulker: You have already spoken of the big, medium and the small muscles, and I can say that I have already tried several times to decontract myself. But I don't see the classification that way. I understand, however, that there are muscles which have no role in exterior movement, but are internal, almost visceral.

Gurdjieff: When you tense the large muscles, the small ones also tense themselves, but you don't see them. But now pay attention: when your large muscles are tense, the medium ones begin to tense, then the small ones too. You then decide to do something different, and there is no longer any need for the small ones to remain tense. The small ones depend on the medium, the medium muscles on the big, and the big on both the small and medium muscles. Even a donkey can decontract its large muscles. But to decontract the small muscles, well that is something beyond a donkey, that is a job for a human cow.

It is impossible to explain this: if by this point you haven't understood it, this proves that you don't relax yourself. You only relax your big muscles. But now, make the acquaintance of your small muscles. These small muscles are not interior. I can isolate them from myself. For example, I can relax a certain part of myself so that even if you stuck me with a needle, I would feel nothing. It's a special fakir preparation. I can relax the small muscles to the point of isolating them from myself. If they are isolated, they have no contact with myself. And if they are not in contact, then no harm is done to me. Such things have a purely local character. Even were I to cut myself, it wouldn't bleed.

Up until the present we have spoken of the muscles in general. But now we're speaking of three classes of muscles. After that, when you're able to understand, I will explain to you, and will prove to you, that in each class of muscle there obtain three different qualities. Even in the large muscles there are three different qualities of realisation. *[To Philippe]* Meanwhile, this will be the first exercise of your fresh start, and I hope that it will produce in you faith in your possibilities of becoming.

Philippe: Without recommencing the separation exercise?

Gurdjieff: Do this one alone: you can return to that exercise later.

Aboulker: I've noticed that when I've done the exercises with great intensity, it's painful not to be able to decontract the throat muscles. I have no power over those muscles, and I cannot decontract them.

Gurdjieff: Maybe your exercises have not been going so well because of that problem. The weakness is there. My opinion is that, as with your comrade, you could leave the other exercises and start once more with this one.

Aboulker: But it's only when I have a certain tension that the muscles contract themselves, and they bother during the exercise. But if I'm doing the exercise of concentration, they leave me in tranquillity.

Gurdjieff: Philippe, among other things, you changed one word. In place of the word "relax," you've substituted the word "decontract."

Relaxation is without end. While there is a limit to decontraction, you can go very far with relaxation. It was you who changed the word. At the same time, if you could understand how you did that, you would understand yet better many of your subjectivities. But this way, you close the door to understanding. This, this is you.

As soon as you started to speak, I said to myself: "It's Philippe speaking." Afterwards, as you continued, it was apparent to me that it was "Philippe" speaking. I wish for you that you could understand the difference, for then you could understand many things in your life which are similar to that manifestation.

Do not forget this: decontraction—even a donkey can do that. But relaxation—only the intellect can do that. May God help you with your intellect (Que Dieu vous aide avec votre intellect). *[To Aboulker]* And you're satisfied too?

Aboulker: Yes monsieur.

Gurdjieff: Mother, may I smoke? *[To J.]* Note this example—she is mother, the mother of the house; you remember what I said the last time, that no one may do anything without the mother's permission. The mother is head (of the house).

[Mr. Gurdjieff jokes about J., says J. is jealous because his mother no longer belongs only to him but to everybody present, and when he loses her he will realise the value of what he possessed.]

Gurdjieff: Eh! After what we have just read about the ceremony of Christ, I think it is difficult for anyone to ask a question. But even so, one must try, even though it be egoistical to ask a question.

Hig: Sir, I'd like to ask a question. Having finished several weeks ago the tasks I had laid out for myself, I find myself since then in a happy balance without a hiatus and without a desire. I wish to go on working because I feel there is a universe above the one where I now am, but I can't make any progress since that time and I feel that alone I can do nothing.

Gurdjieff: It's a bad sign. You must look for a shock from outside. You are contented with little. Now during this period you should make effort. You should be having an interior struggle between your individuality and your functions. You must not calm yourself. The fact that you cannot work is a very good sign. You must force yourself. If you pass this crisis, this small crisis, you can begin again afterwards.

Hig: I don't see exactly what path to follow and what aim to have in view.

Gurdjieff: A path isn't necessary. It is only necessary that you obtain results in yourself. Collect, accumulate the results of struggle. You will need them for continuing. You must accumulate; you have batteries in you in which you must accumulate this substance, like electricity. This substance can only be accumulated by struggle. Therefore create a struggle between your head and your animal. I already explained this the last time. Excuse me. It was Saturday that I told it. My memory is getting old. I never used to make mistakes and now I begin to. I advise you—now that I know you a thousand times better—not to stop. Continue your struggle, but without waiting for results. Accumulate the results of the process of struggle. When we struggle interiorly with thought, feeling and body, that gives a substance in the place where it belongs. We have no interest today in knowing where that place is. Accumulate. It is this that is lacking in you. You are young. You haven't experience. You are empty. Continue the struggle accidentally begun. So that if you say that you are satisfied, that proves you are on the right road. But you must not stop. You had as a plan to go to the Etoile. You are in the Rue d'Armaillé. The Etoile is still far: Boulevard Carnot, there are twenty lampposts, twenty *stations*. Now then, turn to the right. That is the right road. That is to say, continue your struggle. You are searching for the means? What you are doing has no importance. What is necessary is that you must have in you the process of struggle. What means shall you employ? That isn't important. Struggle. You know better than I what struggle. For example, whatever your body likes, whatever you have the habit of giving it, don't give it any more. The important thing is to have a continual process of struggle, because you need the substance that struggle will give you.

Jac: Mr. Gurdjieff, you gave me as a task, for the purpose of remembering myself, that of working with someone who is near to me. And I have noticed, and so has my wife, that this aim has changed our relation, but only to a certain point, and that there was an obstacle that neither she nor I could pass over. And you told her that you would say what to do to get past this obstacle.

Gurdjieff: First, for every parent, one must begin by bringing forward a question; you and your wife have children. Well, if you have children, they create for you special obligations. Living just for yourselves is finished. You should be obliged to sacrifice everything for your children in your ordinary life. At this time you and your wife ought to plan as an aim to live for your children; it is the aim of you and your wife. Nothing should interfere with your mutual relations. You should have this common aim between you. You should have an aim, a common aim, between you, and this common aim between you will give a contact for the work, because it is an objective aim and the work is also objective. Begin this. Discuss it with your wife. With her, plan as an aim to sacrifice everything to your children. Not for always, but for a special period of time. All for your children. Your aim will be a common one. And in your personal relations there will be a struggle, for if you both plan this aim with your minds, since your characters are different each one will have—because each will have chosen his aim—an interior struggle to sustain in himself. And he who will attain this aim will have passed his examination in order to have another objective way [moyen] that will come afterwards. In the meantime speak quietly and frankly with your wife and plan this aim. If you do this for one or two weeks, you will then deserve to know the objective way.

Pom: May I ask a question?

Gurdjieff: If you please. This is the first time you have spoken, isn't it?

Pom: I should like to know what to do to prevent, outside of the work which lasts a certain length of time, my imagination from running away with me.

Gurdjieff: Well, for that I'm going to give you a very simple and very ordinary piece of advice. You too are on the right path. Now what I advise you is a very simple thing. To understand logically can give you absolutely nothing. You will understand afterwards that only this advice is good which I'm about to give you. During all your free time, count: one, two, three, four, five, six, up to fifty. Afterwards: fifty, forty-nine, forty-eight, forty-seven, forty-six, etc., until you are back where you started. All the time. And if you do it seven times, five or ten minutes, sit down, relax and say to yourself: "I am", "I wish to be", "I can be", "not to use it to do evil, but good", "I will help my neighbour when I shall be. I am." After that, count again. But consciously, not automatically. You do that all your free time. The first time it will seem absurd to you. But when you have done it for two or three weeks, you will thank me with all your heart. Have you understood me?

Pom: Very well.

Gurdjieff: I give you nothing else. I know a thousand other things. But I give you this simple thing. *[To the others]* And that will save him. His entire life will change and until the hour of his death he will thank me, he will never forget me. Do that, and that is all.

Mme Et: May I ask you for some advice? I was wanting to ask you: when I do my work of remembering myself, I am always hampered by the same idea: how can I do my work, how can I organise my day, so that everyone in the house is happy? And during the day, it's just the opposite. I am hampered by the ideas that have to do with the work. I think about what I've heard here and at Mme de Salzmann's, and that constantly impedes me.

Gurdjieff: That is the result of the demands of daily living. It happens to everyone. I've often said this. You must set aside a special time each day for the work. Not all the time, the Work is a very serious thing. You cannot work interiorly all day. You must make a special time and increase it little by little. To this work you give a half hour of the twenty-four hours. During this half hour forget all the rest, put all the rest aside. It's a little thing. You sacrifice to this time all your occupations, all the work of your exterior functions. Sacrifice everything for your interior work and afterwards you can put it aside for the things of ordinary life. You cannot do this work all day.

Mme Et: I think so. That becomes mechanical. I am, I wish to be.

Gurdjieff: You mix, you must not. Don't mix this work with ordinary work. We have two kinds of waking states. For this work, you should have one active waking state. But a half hour of this waking state is enough for the rest of the day, which you live as you have the habit of doing. You can do this? And if you can't do a half hour, even ten minutes is rich for him who can work ten minutes. You must give and sacrifice to this work a special time. You cannot give all your time. Life is one thing, the work another. The substantiality of each one is different: for this work you must be more active. I've said this many times. When you begin your work, your task, it is your work. You should, even before beginning, relax yourself, prepare yourself, collect yourself. Afterwards, with all your being, you accomplish your task. It is a very complicated thing. You cannot do it for a long time. You are soon tired. It takes all your strength. If you do it five minutes too much, you are drained of all strength. It's for that reason that I say you must increase the time little by little, until you are used to it: five minutes, six minutes, ten minutes. Only this system will always give you a good beginning to prepare you for acquiring the state that is becoming to a real man. And if you work a long time, that proves that you do not work with all your being—you are working only with your mind. But as to that, you can do it for a thousand years without gaining anything; it is worth nothing. Work a short time, but work well. Here it isn't the quantity but the quality that counts. Life is one thing. Do not mix it with other things. Five minutes of good work is worth more than twenty-four hours of another kind. If you haven't much time, work five minutes. Let ordinary life continue automatically according to habit the rest of the time. What you say does not concern the work. Our life is one thing, the work another thing. Otherwise you will become a psychopath. You remember yourself with your mind—it is worthless; remember yourself with all your being. You can't do it for long, you drain yourself. Do it for five minutes, but forget everything else. Be an absolute egoist, forget everything, your God, your husband, your children, money—remember only the work. Short, but substantial.

[He speaks in Russian with Mme de Salzmann.]

Bar: May I ask a question? How can I distinguish between my mental centre and my physical centre?

Gurdjieff: Take a simple task. When you think, you think. Associations go on automatically; that is your mind. When you feel hot or cold, when you are nervous, angry, when you like, when you don't like—that is your feeling.

Bar: But in one's actions, how can one prevent the centres from encroaching on each other: thinking with my feeling, to have a mental feeling, and to mistake one for the other.

Gurdjieff: You wish to say that you can't think because you are feeling?

Bar: I mean that I have an emotional thought.

Gurdjieff: You have a weakness, a sickness; you must not think with your feeling; you must think with your head. To think with your feeling is a weakness, a sickness. The beginning comes from feeling and the centre of thought is only a function. But the centre of gravity must be the thought. And now you can know what is individuality. It is when your centre of gravity is in your thought. So, if your centre of gravity is not in your thought, you are not an individual, you are an automaton. It's a simple explanation. Every man should try to accustom himself to being an individual, an independent person, something, not *merde* (excuse the word), not an animal, dog, cat. It is a very simple symptom. If you concentrate your being in your thought, you are an individual; there are many degrees among individuals, but that isn't important for the moment. You are an individual when you have your centre of gravity in the thinking centre. And if it is in another centre, you are only an automaton. It can be in your body and in your feeling, but when you work you should always have for aim to be in your thought. And this do consciously. If you do not, everything does itself unconsciously in you. Your work should be exclusively to concentrate yourself in your thought. It's a simple explanation. Phillip? To you also it should explain many things.

Philip: Theoretically I know it.

Gurdjieff: But for your understanding this should have given you something new, some interesting conclusions?

Zu: Sir, I asked you last Thursday, if there was a way to develop attention; you said that attention was measured in the degree that one remembers oneself. You told me to especially look into myself. I especially asked you that because I wasn't able to put my attention on the reading of Beelzebub. During this week I understood that attention was what I was. As many "I's" as there were, so many different attentions. I wanted to ask you if there was, for developing attention, only the method of "I am" or if there are other special methods?

Gurdjieff: One thing I can tell you. Methods do not exist. I do not know any. But I can explain now everything simply. For example, in Beelzebub, I know, there is everything one must know. It is a very interesting book. Everything is there. All that exists, all that has existed, all that can exist. The beginning, the end, all the secrets of the creation of the world; all is there. But one must understand, and to understand depends on one's individuality. The more man has been instructed in a certain way, the more he can see. Subjectively, everyone is able to understand according to the level he occupies, for it is an objective book, and everyone should understand something in it. One person understands one part, another a thousand times more. Now, find a way to put your attention on understanding all of Beelzebub. This will be your task, and it is a good way to fix a real attention. If you can put real attention on Beelzebub, you can have a real attention in life. You didn't know this secret. In Beelzebub there is everything, I have said it, even how to make an omelette. Among other things, it is explained; and at the same time there isn't a word in Beelzebub about cooking. So, you put your attention on Beelzebub, another attention than that to which you are accustomed, and you will be able to have the same attention in life.

[A joke with Pom about tobacco and how to dry it, and then about rice powder and gunpowder; and about the French language which is rich only in the insults between taxi drivers.]

Mme de Salzmann: Really now, has no one anything more to say?

Jac: Mr. Gurdjieff, a little while ago I was very interested by Pom's question and by your answer. In my life which is customarily very bustling and very trivial, I observe how little room there is for the work. All too often I feel myself lost. Which is normal. But what is less normal is that I am attached to, belong to, this bustle, to this triviality which exactly fits me, the ordinary me, the individual who is the strongest in me. And I ask you if I should not apply to my own case the advice which you gave to Pom, because I believe that it contains something clear and simple which will pull me out of the squirrel cage in which I am always turning.

Gurdjieff: That would not do for you at all. It is difficult to count like that: one, two, three, up to fifty. I am going to give you something yet more simple. You have a family. A father? A mother? A brother?

Jac: And a sister.

Gurdjieff: A sister also: five persons. Beginning tomorrow morning, you take as a task: every ten minutes, a little less or a little more, about ten minutes—it's the same to me if it's eight or twelve—remember your father, ten minutes later your mother, etc. You remember them and you represent them to yourself. And when you have finished with the four, ten minutes afterwards "I am", "I wish to be", with the sensing of all your presence; and ten minutes afterwards you begin again—your father, your mother, etc. And like that you pass all your time. It's more simple like that. You understand? By the way, you must have an *idée fixe.* When you think of your mother each fifth time, think that she's here with silver things in her ears, cheap things; and you give your word to yourself that when you are grown up and are earning money, you will take as a task to earn her gold ones. *[To Mme Et.]* Ten percent for me. *[To Jac.]* You have understood me?

77

Bar: Mr. Gurdjieff, when one is seized with a feeling of profound sadness from which one cannot manage to emerge, with what mechanical means can one get away from it?

Gurdjieff: If one doesn't know the cause of it?

Bar: No, one doesn't.

Gurdjieff: There is no such sadness; it is idiocy. Go to see a specialist. I can recommend a neuropathologist. I know him very well, he gives me ten percent.

Bar: Sometimes I notice it after luncheon.

Gurdjieff: Oh, oh, that's a symptom; you eat more than you should. Eat less. Don't eat the last piece, that's all. Do you understand that? You know what it is, the last piece. You understand? Then bravo. Test this and next time we will speak. It's possible the cause of it is there. If it isn't we'll find another way.

[Jokes with Dr. Ab. about medicine.]

Hig: Sir, I'd like to ask another question. I don't understand what conscious love can be. I don't understand why the lucidity with which one examines one's passion and discloses its causes does not at once kill it.

Gurdjieff: Well then, say that love only interests the functions. It is only physical polarity that is working. When you have thought that, love will become repugnant to you. The love that everybody has, you have. But conscious love, that is real love. You have only love based on sex; it is a sickness, a weakness. You cannot have love. That which perhaps your grandfather had. Today, for everyone, love is based on sex and sex on polarity. So if a person has a nose like this you love her; if she hasn't a nose like that, you don't love her. Real love is objective; but in Paris objective love doesn't exist. You have made the word sentiment for sex, for dirty things; you have forgotten real love.

Hig: But must one seek to repress it for the sake of the other?

Gurdjieff: Regard it as a weakness and put it aside. And at the same time, use it for looking at yourself. Profit from everything. And from instinct you will perhaps be able to feel real love. The taste will perhaps come to you. Once you have pity for a person whose nose you don't like, or for another who seems ill, for a child without a mother, for a person who is hungry, for a man without a wife—then, for each person, you will be able to enter his situation. Have contact

78

with your different impulses; and if you remain impartial, you will see that everything you have had in you until now is *merde,* and at the same time you will be able to try to have the taste of another quality of love. And if the taste of it comes to you, I can explain the details to you.

Ab: Sir, in order to experience this conscious love, can polarity be a help or a hindrance?

Gurdjieff: A hindrance, naturally. But you can't do anything about it. You are a slave of this law. Wish or not wish. Your body makes you love or not love. Consciously, you can be no longer the slave of your polarity. But first you must have the taste. All I can say in the meantime is that love exists, objective love. But you must have the taste of it. Afterwards we will speak about it. All that we can say beforehand would remain theoretical. About this, Beelzebub explains many things. Concerning the commandments of Ashiata Shiemash there is this:

Love of consciousness evokes the same in response.
Love of feeling evokes the opposite.
Love of body depends only on type and polarity.

And there is also this about hope:

Hope of consciousness is strength.
Hope of feeling is slavery.
Hope of the body is disease.

And about faith:

Faith of consciousness is freedom.
Faith of feeling is weakness.
Faith of the body is stupidity.

And now, District Attorney, try first to earn a lot; and you, mother, come to see me. I know a place where there are golden things. I have a friend at the pawnshop.

[Reading: Purgatory. Dinner. Mr. Gurdjieff reproaches the director for not having indicated to him the presence of a new person.]

Gurdjieff: And now, someone has perhaps something to say which interests me, so to say, a report, which interests everybody also?

Philippe: I wanted to ask a question.

Gurdjieff [to Luc]: Petit, please. Go now to do the commission which I gave you. Afterwards I will give you the report of the *Procureur. [To Philippe]* And you, you have lost your *camarade.* There again, it is my fault. You begin to speak, and he goes away. I disturb you. I am always acting like the devil. Please, I am waiting.

Philippe: I wanted to ask a question about vanity, why, always at the best moments and at the worst, vanity comes. If one succeeds in doing an exercise, for example, or if one misses it. But in every case there is an opportunity for vanity.

Gurdjieff: It is a very simple thing. Perhaps you had a bad education, a bad preparation? This factor (vanity) has been the only one which you have been given in your education by your parents, your nearest, your friends; this factor, only. And when there comes into you another factor, that first one returns and submerges everything else. To be precise, you must with this constatation become aware that your great enemy is this factor crystallised in you. How you have been educated, of that I know nothing. But perhaps it is your education which made you like this. It put into you this cornerstone. This factor is the foundation stone of your organism. When another factor arrives, another impulse, this first one also functions and as it is stronger it submerges and dominates everything. That is a very good constatation for you and also for him who studies the psyche. For you, doctor, it is very interesting. It is very important this in psychology. Sometimes a quite small thing like that can prevent one from continuing. Objectively it is a very small thing, but for him who subdues it, it is a big enemy, an organic enemy. You can do nothing against it. It is a thousand times stronger than you. All the rest is weak. Your work is weak, this kills everything. It is necessary to reinforce a thousand times your individuality, your I. When it begins to direct your functions, then you will have to try to make "tchik" of your vanity. Today, it is impossible. But struggle to diminish its strength. With "I am" or factors like that, parallel to "I am." Allow these factors to crystallise in you, and automatically the other factor can diminish. Among other things (and this is between ourselves) your question helps me very much to understand you. Now I know which is your enemy, what dog you have, and I shall be able better to guide you. Meanwhile do what I told you to do until today, and I will give you henceforth many exercises for the general functioning.

Among other things, in truth, it is the books of *bon ton*, the books of education which taught you that this factor was necessary in life. It is inculcated into children; the one who educated you did everything to crystallise vanity in you. He never thought that one day when you were grown-up, you would choose another road. And it is very difficult to change one's road. If you had kept to the first road, it would have been a very good thing for you, this vanity. If you had been an official, a civil servant, a minister, an officer of the guards, it would have been excellent. But for a normal life, it is your dog number one. Today, mark this day like an anniversary. Even I, up to the present perhaps, I had not understood you and I could not give you exact reasons for your inner confusion. And now, I see everything. Your interior is illuminated for me like a picture; you have helped me to help you.

Mme D: Mr. Gurdjieff, in these last two weeks I made a more sustained effort than before and I have tried to act in such a manner in life that the "I" is separated from the "me" to be able better to carry out the difficulties of life as an external role which I have to carry out without being touched inside. This has helped me very much to understand voluntary suffering better and I have seen that in the moments when I was able to feel the "I," I was able to face everything that was happening to me. But I saw also that I had continuously to try to feel it. Because it didn't last very long. The memory of it lasted more than ever before, but to feel it lasted very little.

Gurdjieff: Wait, do not continue. I have already understood very well. And I am going to ask Mme de Salzmann, by exception, to explain to you the exercise number one of Saturday. *[To Mme de Salzmann]* It will save her, it will make things easy for her. Only this exercise can help her. *[To Mme D.]* This exercise will help you to understand in a very definite manner. This exercise will separate "you" from "yourself." You know what man is made of: of individuality and of functions of the organism. Until now, in you the two things existed like a single one, one function mixed with the other, one function interfering with the other. When we separate the interior life from the exterior life, "I" is the interior, "me" is the exterior, and it is possible to separate them in a definite manner. This exercise will help you to do that. Afterwards, you will be able to know and you will be responsible for your future. Till now, you were not responsible. You will be. You will know, and it will be your fault if you do not act well. Sufferings of all sorts will be necessary to square your debt. Go then to Mme de Salzmann. She will explain. Do what she tells you for two weeks and I will answer your question.

Mr. A: I wanted to ask you a question which is similar to P's, but what happens to me is not vanity, it is the wish that people have a good opinion of me.

Gurdjieff: It is the same thing. It is the same factor: showing off.

Mr. A: But, Mr. Gurdjieff, even if it brings me nothing? Even if it is useless?

Gurdjieff: It is the same thing.

Mr. A: Mr. Gurdjieff, I asked you a similar question a year ago or a little more than a year, when I came to you for the first time. But since, it has not changed at all.

Gurdjieff: You had not the possibility. You had not the factors. It is different now.

Mr. A: Now it is less apparent. Before, everyone could see it. But now it is more subtle. The only change, it is in the manner of looking for that good opinion, I have become much more subtle.

Gurdjieff: Why do you say that? You have only constated it. Before acting like a normal person, you have noticed that you were an abnormal person. Your impartial reason noticed it. It is not more subtle but it appears so.

Mr. A: It dirties everything I do.

Gurdjieff: Evidently. It gives emanations. Of a yellow colour, for instance. And as it is the strongest factor in you, it gives this yellow colour to all your functions. I tell you the same thing. You must crystallise consciously in yourself another factor stronger than this one. Already you have much material. For example, "I am." When one begins to work with "I am," one succeeds in killing this manifestation. If one starts again a hundred times, then it will be able to transform itself; today this is your "me." If you crystallise another stronger factor, this first factor will become a simple function again. But this factor of vanity is very good, it must not be killed. It is necessary only that it never has the initiative, it must never enter into your "I." It must remain a function, and when it is necessary, send for it like a function.

Mr. A: But if I send for it, it takes all the room; it is that which is dangerous.

Gurdjieff: We speak for the future. We repair the past, we work. You have not yet experienced that. I explain it to you for your work and that is all. With this work, you can repair your past and prepare your future. It is exactly the same thing as P. Only, the outside is a little different. That also is the *merde* education, the *fou-fou* education. (Call it how you like, I only say one word: *merde*. I speak bad French, so I call everything which is bad *merde*.) Everyone has this education here. And specially in France, I noticed that in a very original experience. I always have bonbons in my pocket. When I see a child I give some to it. With a child there is always someone, father, mother, aunt. Without exception they all say the same thing to the child: "What do you say?" Automatically, little by little, the child says thank you to everyone and feels nothing any more. This is idiot thing. This is *merde*. When a child wishes to say thank you to me, I understand it. It speaks a language which I understand. And it is that language which I love. Only to hear it, only to see its impulses, I spend every day five kilos on bonbons, for which I pay four hundred and ten francs a kilo. Only to see these impulses. But when one says to a child: "What do you say?" one kills everything. It is merde, father, mother. They kill the child for the future, and they kill my goodwill. It is a good example, this, you know. I don't know how you understand it, but for me it is very characteristic. I say it as example. People prepare everything automatically, they make children function like bells which ring when one presses them, like an electric push-button. One presses one button or the other.

Mr. A: On the other hand, one lives in society. There are conventions which even children have to learn.

Gurdjieff: Then, remember exactly how I said, I said it is necessary to be free inside and not identify, and externally play a role. Myself, for instance, I am old, I am seventy-six, I play my role: all the children love me, all the mothers, the grandmothers, the fathers, all love me. I play my role. But objectively for me all that is merde, inside. It is my experimenting. For me they are mice. I live here. They are my mice. If I lived in another section, it would be other mice. I did not say that the children must change externally, but I said that inside one must not identify. Each class must be educated to play a corresponding role, this is the ideal. But, inside, it is necessary to be free, without identifying oneself. It is that which is necessary. It is a very little thing. And after that life is a bed of roses. After that, some time when you are on the bed of roses, you can work with pleasure for your future. But now you have not much pleasure. *Procureur,* it would interest me very much to hear one thing. Your future relations with me depend on one question. This question now, it is perhaps the moment to put it on the table. Can your mother say that during these last weeks, one or two weeks, you have really changed, five to ten percent, and that her nervousness has diminished? Not much, five to ten percent. I ask that. It is very important for me to know that.

Mme E: Yes, Monsieur, I can say it. They have changed much.

Gurdjieff: Not much. Much I don't know, five to ten percent.

Mme E: So much changed both of them that I would not recognise them.

Gurdjieff [to J.]: I thank you. Now you can count on me.

Mme E: Mr. Gurdjieff, I would like to ask you a question. When one sees a truth late in one's life, one must look back, and one sees that many things in one's life should have been otherwise and one feels remorse and even sorrow. Should one throw out this remorse or on the contrary keep it and make use of it?

Gurdjieff: You have perhaps a big opportunity. You have an experience. If you have constated what you have just said, you can prepare yourself for your future. Perhaps you have a thousand times more chance than a younger person. I congratulate you. You have many possibilities for the future. Not for the present. The present which is the result of the past, for I cannot repair your past. You would have to have many years for that. But if now you put this past in order, I take responsibility for your future. Mother, I am very pleased with your sons. *[To J.]* I am doubly pleased with you. And with your brother too. *[To A.]* With you, too. You are two shoes of the same pair.

Mlle D: Mr. Gurdjieff, I would like to ask you. My greatest difficulty for my self-remembering is the mind, which is never right. I never succeed in decontracting it, in resting it. It happens that I do not believe it. But when it is in motion, it has heaps of associations in which I do not believe but which absorb me. That creates a duality which is very painful for me.

Gurdjieff: We have spoken about dogs. Among all your dogs that is your dog; you have many of them in you.

Mlle D: Can I, for instance, in life, when I ride a bicycle, try to occupy my mind?

Gurdjieff: Try. Try what helps you. In your attempts there must be a struggle. Try everything. But there must always be a condition in it: that it is always struggle between your thought and your body. With this process, if you try you can find.

Mlle D: I tried to do the exercise of counting up to fifty. It brought me nothing.

Gurdjieff: Try something else. That perhaps does not correspond to your subjectivity. Try a thousand things, search, think. I already gave you two things, but I can give a third. You have a brother?

Mlle D: Not here.

Gurdjieff: But in general.

Mlle D: Yes.

Gurdjieff: Then do an exercise.

Mlle D: But they are not in Paris.

Gurdjieff: It is not important. They are on the earth, they are not on Mars, so that will do. For instance, you think of your brother. One is always a big enemy for one's sister or for one's brother. It is the normal education of today which wishes that. On the contrary, you do an exercise. You represent to yourself your brother. You with a photo. Inside you wish for him good luck, and for your sister you wish for her a difficult enough present that she may have a good future. Do the exercise as a good service, as a work and nothing else. Do that. *[To Mme E.]* You understand that a bad present can give a good future? That has the appearance of an absurd wish. But at the same time, you understand, mother, don't you?

Mr. M: Mr. Gurdjieff?

Gurdjieff: Show your nose first.

Mr. M: I have often heard you use this expression: that God disposes so that the devil takes you and that the devil disposes so that God takes you. I would like to know how to reconcile these two things and what measures to take to know when it is necessary for God to take you or the devil.

Gurdjieff: That is an objective question. You have not the subjective data to understand this objective question. It is curiosity. You have a thousand questions more important for your subjectivity. That is objective, it is much too soon for you, you have not in you the factor to understand that.

[Mr. Gurdjieff talks in Russian to Mme de Salzmann.]

Mme de Salzmann: Mr. Gurdjieff says that there are a thousand subjective questions which arise for you and which you must resolve before you ask about God and the devil. You must not be interested in these things. It is abstract, it is curiosity.

Gurdjieff: I am not there to satisfy your curiosity, my time is too expensive.

Mme D: Would you be kind enough to give me some advice how to give a good education to the children who are entrusted to us, such as we are?

Gurdjieff: You ask Mme de Salzmann to give you two chapters of a book I have written. "My Father" and "My First Tutor". I have explained there briefly what you ask me. These two chapters will give you some good instruction.

Mme D: Because I have already modified my way of teaching since I came here. But I am often in difficulties, I think I have noticed that children are sensitive to the efforts which one makes to remember oneself; also, what I can best do is to struggle against the big negative emotions. It seemed to me that the children were sensitive to it.

Gurdjieff: A thousand times more than you. In children crystallisation is a thousand times more than in you. That is the danger of suggesting something bad to a child whose sensitiveness is a thousand times stronger than yours.

Mme D: I have less difficulty in remembering myself in class in front of children than at other times.

86

Gurdjieff: Your children do not emanate yet.

Mme D: It seems to me that the children are calmer. Before, when they were nervous, I shouted to calm them. Now I try to be calm and in their turn the children get calm automatically.

Gurdjieff: You have constated a good thing. It is not your teaching which matters for the future of the children, it is your emanations. Not for the present, for the future. You can only teach automatic associations but your emanations are important and show how much unconscious education is harmful.

Mme D: I have noticed that a class is a caricature of the teacher and that one can know him through the atmosphere of his class.

Gurdjieff: You have made some very good observations. Observe again and you can know yourself through the children. Think egoistically that you work for the moment for yourself. What I do I do to be able to be a good altruist later. Today I am merde altruist. I wish to be a good egoist to put myself well on my feet.

Mme D: I wanted also to ask your precise advice. My little boy wishes to affirm himself more and more. He always says no and he is always opposing. To make him give up, I have two means. Either to speak to him a long time, to reason with him, which is not always possible: Or to distract him, to give him a plaything, which is very easy, but which does not seem to me very good.

Gurdjieff: The second is bad and the first is good. Reason with him, using analogies; children like analogies very much.

Mme D: But it is difficult.

Gurdjieff: That is another question. You must do it. The second means you must not use. The child understands very well, it is more intelligent than the grown-ups, but it needs a very simple logic. What it has understood it never forgets.

Mme D: It is very difficult for us.

Gurdjieff: But it is very easy for it. For us it is difficult but for a child it is very easy to understand a good explanation. It is difficult for you to explain because you have been badly educated. You have been educated not to be a teacher, but for knitting socks. And now, there you are, a teacher and I, I have holes in my socks.

S: Mr. Gurdjieff, I have always been extremely careless.

[Discussion with Mme de Salzmann on the word careless and its translation.]

Gurdjieff: Say you are careless. But that I have known for a long time. Tell us something new.

S: I see it better now and I see how it is serious in all fields. And till now, although I see it, I had not undertaken the struggle against it, because it led me too far away. But today I wanted to struggle because this carelessness leads me away always and I ask you what to do.

Gurdjieff: Fix for yourself a task specially on that. As this factor is very strong in you, you must find a very strong measure. You smoke?

S: No.

Gurdjieff: You eat?

S: Yes.

Gurdjieff: Then fix for yourself a task on that. Do not be careless. And if you notice that you have been careless, the same day, you give yourself your word not to eat the next meal. Till the next meeting. If you do struggle you eat. If you do not struggle, you do not eat. It is the only measure, there is no other one.

[Notice: If you are a guest somewhere this rule does not count. It is only at home that you don't eat.]

R: How is it that ideas in which you believe and of which you are convinced do not penetrate profoundly into you, but remain on the surface and do not affect your life?

Gurdjieff: Because you are convinced at the moment when you speak, but afterwards you go into life.

R: But afterwards in life one does other things from those of which one is convinced. I act against what I believe.

Gurdjieff: Because you have an education of this kind. Your education is like that. We have two independent organisms. One is the result of our preparation, the other is our body at the beginning. This body can only function when I am relaxed, quiet and alone. When I enter into life, it is weak. I cannot do any more and it is the other which gets the better of me. I cannot do any more what I decided and it is thus that you go on doing what you have the habit of doing. You have an idea. Before manifesting yourself in life, when you are alone in the house, you relax yourself and you make a programme; how you must manifest yourself during the day. Then, you suggest to yourself to follow your programme exactly. You fall, ten times, twenty times. The first twenty times you fall, the twenty-first time you can do what you have decided to do when you are alone. There is no other means for the moment. Make a programme in the state which I advised you. Make yourself quiet, calm, relaxed. Then for your near future, you make this programme. You enter in life and you try to do as you have decided. If you do it very well, you give yourself something nice. And if you forget you punish yourself.

R: One has not enough force of will to punish oneself.

Gurdjieff: You must accustom yourself. That gives force for the future. You struggle and this struggle gives results little by little, it accumulates them for you. You fall once, ten times, but each struggle gives results, like a substance which accumulates in you and the results of these accumulations help me to accomplish a conscious decision. All that is ordinary. But to have other things, it is necessary to have material, it is necessary to know. It is the first time you are here. There are a thousand different exercises. But for the first time you are here I explain it to you in general, with ordinary things. There are other things to say but one cannot say everything at once. There are other exercises which we have done but it is necessary to proceed little by little. Your aim is the aim for everyone here.

[Mr. Gurdjieff asks for news of René Daumal; drinks to the health of all wise men, jokes on the wise men and roses, and nicknames Pomereu the nephew of Uncle Sam.]

*[Lecture: The work of the saints of Ashiata Shiemash. Dinner. Jokes
with Miss Gordon and Boussique on peeling raisins.]*
   Hignette: Mr. Gurdjieff, I would like to ask you a question.
   Gurdjieff: Excuse me, please, can you wait? I want to say some-
thing to this Monsieur.
   [Indicates Jacques Baratier.]
   Today I can verify something. I know him, I have seen him more
than once and at the same time I was not sure that it was really him.
It seemed to me that it was not him. That never happens to me. I
photograph people. But in my head this photo of him was only half-
clear and for several days I said to myself: "Why is this?" Today I
understand.
   Baratier: Why, Mr. Gurdjieff?
   Gurdjieff: I see your brother over there; I knew not that he was
here. I believed that your brother was you and you were you. I had
not fixed your brother. But today I see you independently, one on
the left, the other on the right; you have nothing in common
exteriorly, but in essence you are very similar. One can wager that it
is the same father. Why is everyone laughing? What I say is very
normal.
   Ha! Enough. Today is Thursday and at the same time, Thursday
which begins in a new way. It is the Thursday of a sequence of
Thursdays that will be of a new quality. The Thursdays before are
dead. We can never more start over. It is a different quality of
Thursday, with more details. Among others, for this Thursday,
several people have said to me: "I cannot fulfil the condition, which
has been laid down, to interest and to bring seven people to the
work." I had laid down as a condition that only those would come
on Thursdays who hoped to be able to bring and to interest seven
new people, without explaining to them anything strange about the
ideas, interesting them only with the ideas, my ideas, with that
which he has studied here, done here, the tools which we have
given him and nothing else. Seven persons in six months. That was
the first condition. And certain ones have made of me this inquiry:
and I reply that he is an idiot who questions me thus. It is not a

question of bringing seven people in six months; for if truly one interests a single person in coming, this person can help you in bringing fourteen. It is not difficult. It is not a question of seven. One is enough to begin. Only it must be a person who shall have been really started, well begun, who could interest himself in our ideas. And automatically he shall be able to assist you, you shall be then, you, like a French president—that is to say, you will have nothing to do. He will do everything. *[To Hignette]* Now, my dear, what did you wish?

Hignette: I found myself too calm and too happy; without desire to continue, like stagnant water. And yet, I felt that I must do something. I chose an intellectual and primitive task, and especially under unpleasant conditions. I find myself now extremely tired. And more, that does not accord with my work. I would like to sleep twenty hours a day if I could. I would like to know now how to diminish my task, I no longer have the possibility of that and I do not want it, but how to bear it better and to rest better.

Gurdjieff: In general your work goes well?

Hignette: Intellectually, yes.

Gurdjieff: Then, if yes, do only one thing. The rest I am going to give to you. I am going to give you some pills which you shall take twice a day, morning upon awakening, and night upon going to bed. But you, on your part, each morning when you get up, wash yourself with cold water, then get warm again by doing gymnastics. Do only this; the pills and this. This will change everything in three days. And you will see that your fatigue was imaginary. How can you be tired? You are still young; you have not consumed the reserves of your accumulators. It is psychic. Do this: wash, dry well and take your pills. If you feel nothing in three days (nothing the first day but better the second already, and the third, well) you may come to my house and spit in my face.

One thing adds to this fatigue; it is an intermittent obsession. It is either hope or regret of a person about whom I can only think, and that occasionally during some hours. There is, therefore, nothing to explain; you must do what I tell you. But at the same time rightly, these things demand an explanation which can serve the whole world; thus, I am going to explain it for you and at the same time for everyone. You remember that often I say that you must be internally free. You understand what it is to be free. To identify with nothing. The most important part of our slavery is dependent upon factors which are crystallised in us and which are related to outsiders, to relationships with people unfamiliar to us. And in order to be able to be free, the first work in esoteric schools of all times, begins exactly with this question: "To decrystallise all the factors which are permitted by relations with others" (exceptions made of the crystallised factors which are concerned with persons of the same blood, father, mother, sister, brother, etc., it is the same blood, the same family, the factors must continue). But all the other factors must be decrystallised; you must be an absolute egoist. All love, all respect for whomever it may be you must liquidate; it is necessary that love be transformed into hatred. You must specially influence yourself and work in order to never have close union with anyone. You must neither love nor esteem internally, nor have any sympathy or antipathy. I say *internally*, not externally. Externally you must play your role. But not internally. Everyone who is strange to you, you must reject, save persons of the same blood. Struggle in all ways.

You know yourselves better than I; you know how to influence yourselves and what thoughts and sentiments it is necessary to resist in order to decrystallise these factors. You begin accordingly, and if you see that you cannot, I will help you and I will tell you what you must do. The truth remains the truth. All those who are engaged in internal work must keep no factor of contact, good or bad, whatever it may be; one must be free, completely free from contacts with strangers. I repeat, except for persons of the same blood. For them, one must take no measures to change those qualities of relation. We must not change our contact with our fathers, mothers, etc. One shall change only the form of contact for our fathers, mothers, uncles etc. It is the same blood. Strangers are of another blood; another source; internally they must, to us, be completely indifferent. One must be free of them. Without any slavery. Externally, you can play a role and do what it is necessary to do. That is your business. Man must strive to not identify internally and to play a role externally.

Luc: But if one forbids oneself sympathy towards everybody, will there not be here in us a sentiment which is lacking, notably in the impulsions of remorse, which to us may restore our past and which are an important factor of the work?

Gurdjieff: For this, people of the same blood will suffice you. You have committed many errors towards them; it is to them that your remorse of conscience must go.

Luc: But I have no family.

Gurdjieff: Even one person is sufficient. In your past life, you can make use of much material for the remorse of conscience, towards this person. *[To Hignette]* In that case, now, if we analyse, what reasons did you have for asking your question? The reason is that you have had a contact with someone, a contact of type of polarity. One must struggle all the more, you must use this struggle for your work. Kill in yourself the factors which have permitted this contact with a strange person if he is strange. If he is of your blood, do not touch here for that is another thing. If you have not understood me, talk to Mme de Salzmann. I have explained to her all that was necessary.

Hignette: I would like above all to have something concrete, and how to free myself of a haunting image?

Gurdjieff: Do that which you do for many other things. Be seated, be tranquil, relax carefully. Then you begin to suggest to yourself as to a strange person. With your consciousness, you explain to your subconsciousness that all *that* is slavery and that it is idiotic to have contact with whomever it may be. You explain it as to a stranger. Then you explain it to yourself. One time, ten times you explain it to yourself. And, you should be able, in fact, to receive like a stranger these things which I am going to tell you and which you shall tell yourself. Like a stranger to whom one explains ten times the same thing. Because, your individuality and your body are exactly like you and another person, a stranger. For you, your body is a strange person, the difference being that it is easier to punch someone who is near than someone who is far. Now, your body is nearer; it is thus easier. Not once, but ten times a day, you can talk to yourself.

All must do differently in this work; even sacred compulsions must be killed by yourselves. He who wants to have liberty must kill everything in himself. Even if you love God or Notre Dame, you must kill it in yourself. Even the fused ideas of believing in a saint, you must send it to the devil and the saint will have nothing against you for that.

Luc: I am very surprised by what you say. Because I, who pride myself on having had many contacts in my life, I perceived fifteen days ago, and I am worried, that I no longer feel anything for anyone in relations with people. I am absolutely dry and indifferent, all the while continuing to do the things that I must do and while giving the maximum of myself in my human relations.

Gurdjieff: And you think that you have arrived at that yourself?

Luc: It is the result of the work.

Gurdjieff: But perhaps have I done something special for you, for you to arrive at that? (He believes that he has become like that, completely naturally.) I made of you a special candidate for the work. I have done it purposely. As if I have given you a pill. You are changing and I am content.

Luc: I spoke to someone who told me that he never perceived love for anyone. His head ruled him. Then I did not know how to answer, because I am stricken with the same inability. Something is weak in me.

Gurdjieff: Why do you recall this person?

Luc: In relation to the work.

Gurdjieff: Advice will not help you. Your will is not sufficient to change you, you must have an external aid.

Luc: I am sure of it.

Gurdjieff: I told this young man that it is half-half, on the one hand the external aid: I am going to give him some pills, on the other hand, he himself must wash in cold water and do gymnastics. The pills alone cannot help you. The exercise alone cannot help you without the pills. The two together will change you in one or two weeks.

Alain: There is an impulsion which I am trying to cultivate for my work and which I believed good. It was to search for a clear logical intelligence, by logic, that my body obeys. I had a special way. My detached thought of my personal work. And I found per moment an inclination or rather a surprise of existing, that I believed to be able to intensify in order that it might aid me in being able to give a more powerful effort in recalling. But I understand that it is outward, that the work is separated into two; that the first part of the work gives more strength in proportion as one does it, and I ask myself if it is

94

good to continue.

Gurdjieff: I can tell you one thing. We have a property. If you are on a good path, nature puts immediately in you an idea; she crystallises in you the exact factor that is going to calm you in order to prevent you from continuing on the good way. The more you are on the right way, the more nature uses of these things. It is thus in life. You shall do this therefore: you shall become calm in a good state; you shall sit, very tranquilly (you shall do this for one or two weeks of a month). And you no longer believe anything or anyone. You make a programme. When you have no programme, anything, no matter what idiocy, what worthlessness, what rot, can rule you. Have confidence only in the programme that you shall have made in a special state. The principle thing is to make this programme: how you want to behave, what you want to do, the relations that you want to have with everyone; this is a programme. And you believe only in this. And even if God comes to disturb you and to tell you to do something else, you believe Him not. Perhaps he has come rightly in order to play you a dirty trick. You do only that which you have decided in your special state.

Alain: But it is difficult to believe that the movement of thought will suffice to bring about the much sought after fire, the impulsion.

Gurdjieff: Then you shall lose yourself always; you will always be in your own way. It is the dog, the devil which nature puts in you. Because of this, you believe nothing. Even God you send to the devil. You do not believe in God. But only in the programme that you have decided on. You understand that I am saying an important thing. This state cannot come often. But one can have it once or twice a month; seated, calmly, you realise your three kinds of muscles and after you think absolutely impartially. You consider your state, your class, your character, and how to do all that you have to do in the months that are going to follow. What relations, for example, you want to have with this man or that woman. The programme laid out, you enter into life and you do only that which corresponds to your programme. In life there are thousands of people who want to rule you. You send the whole world to the devil; you believe only in your programme and in your own decision. It is the only exact way for you; the others do not exist, no other way exists; for there are many dogs which nature puts in us expressly to make us weak. Nature is perhaps interested in there being few men on the right path.

Lanctin: Monsieur, until several months ago, I tried to free myself from external influences and in particular in my relation with others. But I have run up against a rather grave obstacle, the difficulty of establishing a relationship with people. I see well what I ought to ask them, but when I am in contact with them, I do not see what they can ask me and I can never make other than a superficial contact.

Gurdjieff: Then, hurry up and expect nothing of the work. It is only after that you will be able to have results. Do everything without identifying yourself internally and, externally, play a role. This role is to be exactly as you were before. Act around each as you have done until now, without letting him know externally that you are working. No one must notice that you do something. Expect nothing. Do only your task. Do not identify internally with anyone or anything. This is your task. Be exactly as before, it is the role that you must play. Automatically you have changed and you cannot be as you were before; this will make you understand what this is and understand why I call this "to play a role." Do not let him see that you are doing something exceptional. Search not to enlighten, to send rays outside, you are not strong enough; you have not the possibility of doing it. One must never expect; leave things to be done as before. Your friend was idiotic? Let him be idiotic, and keep the same relationship. He was intelligent? Let him be intelligent. Show him that nothing has changed. This is called playing a role.

Lanctin: To tell the truth, I had understood this for the old relations that I knew. But for the new, I did not know them before and I do not know how to establish my role.

Gurdjieff: It is yet easier. You remember how you were six months previously and you do as you would have done six months earlier. Not more, not less. You remember how you would have been with her six months ago; and what you have gained, you hide it from her. When everything shall have been decrystallised you will be able to be a new person. I have said a million times not to use that which you have gained; today, be content to work and expect nothing. And if you have gained something, do not use it in life. It is a serious task that you must accomplish; that no one notices that you are something. Not only must one do it, but even as a task, as a special work, without erring. You must do it like a task, to continue to do that which you did before.

Philippe: Just now, in speaking of the family, you enumerated the father, mother, uncle, but not the wife and the children; are they of the same blood? The children are the same blood, but the wife?

Gurdjieff: It is the same blood if you have children because the blood is then mixed with that of the wife. But if you marry and you do not have children, it is not your blood, and you can send your wife to the devil. If you have children, she is of your family. With children the relations must be completely different; the whole world knows that. The bloods are mixed when there are children.

In that which concerns children, it seems better to decrystallise certain factors, certain weaknesses, about a child.

If you work you must work on your weakness: your weakness consists in thousands of things. For example, your child draws always on your amour propre; automatically, you do not love it. This must not exist. If you work, all your work must have the same value for you. These little things prove to me that you work not on yourself; you make differences between your children.

One of your children, for example, touches unconsciously one of your weaknesses. Because of this you can arrive at detesting it; this child, little by little, begins to offend you; in continuing, if this repeats itself, it can crystallise in you some factors of hatred; and if these factors continue to crystallise, it can happen that a father kills his son. His worst enemy can be his son. You must do your work. Your children must have the same value for you. All are your blood. Through them you can have a contact with your wife. There exists, pertinent to this, in Asia an original thing. Over there one calls the wife Fatma. But when she has a child, her husband calls her Padgi, that is to say "sister," and the wife calls her husband Kardavate, that is to say, "brother." They are named brother and sister, they are no longer husband and wife. It is absurd and at the same time it teaches. And this comes to us from very remote times.

Philippe: If a child has horror that the father embrace the mother or touches her arm in front of him, one must avoid it and not touch his mother in front of him?

Gurdjieff: Yes.

Phillipe: And it is right that this be very strong in the child?

Gurdjieff: I am going again to explain to you among other things, something oriental. When a child arrives, after this moment the father and mother must figure that life is finished for them; their life, their satisfactions, all is sacrificed for their children. They do everything for their children and refuse themselves everything. They are father and mother, their life is finished. Their aim is their child; they must do all for him, even kill, even steal, some bad actions—for their children.

Le Prudhomme: There is a question on the same subject that I want to ask you. Our attitude towards one another. We have to act among ourselves in the teaching as with the people outside?

Gurdjieff: Here, it is not the same thing. Here there are comrades. You can make a compromise with your conscience. You know that the first commandment is that the hand wash the hand. Do you understand? If the right hand does not wash the left, the left does not wash the right. If the right doesn't do this *[Mr. Gurdjieff makes a gesture of washing his hands]*, the left hand does not do that. If you don't do good to your comrades, your comrades will not do good to you. If you do good, they are obliged to help you.

Le Prudhomme: Because for me my comrades have become kindred and more dear than my family.

Gurdjieff: It is because you need them, but you must not be a slave.

Le Prudhomme: It is a privilege that I have never felt.

Gurdjieff: But without sentiment, without identification; it is the thought that must be like that.

Le Prudhomme: I cannot distinguish it.

Gurdjieff: But with your consciousness, you must not be slavish; that which is good today, can tomorrow be bad. Tomorrow a comrade can behave towards you as to a stranger. And that your sister cannot do. Doctor, I shall talk with you in a week. I am sure that you will agree with; and you, Mme Dubeau, you can do some good work for me if you follow the advice of the mirror.

Question: I never do a task thoroughly. I think about it, I do it, but only for a second. I cannot hold a thought or a feeling.

[A "task" evidently means one of Mr. Gurdjieff's exercises.]

Gurdjieff: You forget, you have no memory. You forget, you must repeat, repeat, repeat. You wish to say that you have no power of concentration. It is the same with everybody. This is the aim of the work. If a man could really concentrate for a quarter of an hour only, he would be bigger than your Notre Dame, than Christ. I should ask him to be my teacher. If everybody could do this, everybody would be saints. In three centuries there have been perhaps one and a half saints. You must try to achieve gaining perhaps one second a month by repeating, repeating, repeating.

Question: When I see a negative emotion, I see very clearly that it is not the object that counts. It does not exist, it is the covering. As soon as I have seen it, it disappears but the negative emotion remains and becomes occupied with another object, no matter which, then something else. I have noticed the same negative emotions come back again and again by association and they seem to correspond to a tendency. By seeing them, can I think of them as "I's"?

Gurdjieff: Not so many complications. For example, you are hungry. There are different kinds of hunger; the hunger of the morning, of midday, of the evening. They are not the same. The English eat a lot in the morning, the French at night. You have the opportunity to have this material. It is ready made for you. Others will have to make it.

Mme de Salzmann: Through negative emotion one knows something which one cannot know without having it. Envy, fear, anger, etc. One must separate this from oneself so that it does not remain in the essence and can be used when necessary by remaining apart.

Question: I see how empty I am, full of small mundane desires, contradictions like a mill where everything comes in and goes out. I have no will and I have no remedy for this. I lack force.

Gurdjieff: The task has been given for that. If you do not do the task, then let yourself go, open a vein, it will be easier. I can give you a pill to make you sleep forever. A pill is cheap to sleep well alone. One night is much more expensive. If one sleeps well for one night, one can then have a good waking state.

Question: When I see my nothingness, I am completely discouraged. Then to see that I have seen it gives me back hope and great satisfaction of myself. Should I allow myself this?

Gurdjieff: No. Look, always learn to see more and more. Search back into your past. Into your whole life. Suffer for all your failures. Tell yourself you are already twenty-five, that it is too late to do anything; that time is measured. Even when one is one year old, it is already late. Always see your mistakes more and repair.

Question: I see myself in my dreams with such clarity, with such force and disgust that it wakes me up.

Gurdjieff: I spent fifteen years learning not to dream. One must not dream, one must do. There are two states; sleep and a state of waking. When one sleeps, one must sleep. Take a cold shower, give yourself a vigorous rubdown, stand for ten minutes with arms extended and you will sleep. If one sleeps well, one watches well. If one dreams, everything is done by halves. Associations never stop until the end. This is life. But one can stop paying attention to associations. The dreams or associations which continue are those which are the most habitual and therefore which recur. There is also (the book) the Key of Dreams and the Models of Love Letters. You can choose.

Question: Only my head participates in the exercises. How can I avoid this?

Gurdjieff: The head is only the director. It is the policeman with his truncheon who shows the way. One must sense and feel. Work on feeling, on sensing yourself. "I—am," "me—am." Not only your head—the whole man. Repeat, repeat, repeat. Exercises, exercises, thousands and thousands of times. Only this will bring results.

Question: How should one understand "repair the past"? Is it by remorse?

Gurdjieff: You are too complicated. It is much more simple. The present is the result of the past. If you have acquired a bad habit in the past, you must stop it. I see that I have the habit of always turning my thumbs in the same direction. Stop. This is repairing. Do not make the same error again and prepare for the future, prepare for the future. Practise, practise as you would to play the piano. You must develop the strength of your fingers. Repeat, repeat.

Question: I see how I spend hours a day occupied with very small paltry feelings, very vile. Should I attach myself to a task to remedy this, or is there anything else to be done?

Gurdjieff: It is the same for everybody. It has always been so. For you, it is only now that you see this. This is what we wish to change. Do everything that you do well. Even eating. If you eat well, you pray well. Be wholehearted in everything you do. One must work precisely on something precise. Work should not be a desire, but a need, a need. When it becomes a need, you will have an answer. You have not the right to have desire only. This is not enough. It will give nothing. Create a need in yourself. Repeat, repeat, repeat. You never repeat enough. Everything that comes easily to you, make "tchik" [destroy]. Choose something which costs you something, which is an effort. That which is easy is bad for your interior life.

The Aim. Always have an immediate aim. This is your objective. You must achieve this. There are many zigzags on the way. Do not delay. Always see the aim. Know where you are going and you will find the means to get there. Later I will indicate another aim. You must attain the first one first; the aim should be clear and always before you.

Question: When I try to work on remorse, there is always some part of me that refuses, that tells me that it is useless, that it will not lead anywhere or to anything. I wish to understand better the use of remorse, it's necessity, to enable me to convince myself and struggle against this refusal.

Gurdjieff: It is very simple. Look at this.

[He takes a section of a tangerine from his plate.]

This is destined to become jam, it has to become jam, it was made for that. But it is full of salt. What should be done? It must be washed, soaked, cleaned to remove the salt. Afterwards it can become jam. With the salt it is impossible. Remorse is that which removes the salt. This is what purifies. You understand.

Question: When I take my class I have to stop for a moment to collect myself. It seems to me empty, useless, vain. How can I prevent this?

Gurdjieff: You must make your obligations enter into your work. Everything that you do must become a part of your work. This must be your task. Your class must be part of your task. Your task is to help. You must not see the children in their manifestations, but in their future. You must wish to help that future. You must put yourself in their place. Remember how you were at their age. Then you will make them see differently. When you think "I am" at the same time wish to help. You will see then how the children will love you. You will then be able to tell them to go kill their fathers and mothers and they will do it. It will be nothing for them. I have seen this over there with real Masters [Magi]. This is the yeast of the work, the children. It is an opportunity for you. You must become a good labourer.

Question: When I try to put myself in someone's place, there is always one part of me which refuses, which does not participate, which hides, which is occupied with itself and which has enjoyment with itself. It is something which slips away and which I cannot catch. On the other hand, as soon as I have a small result in my work, vanity takes hold of it—"It is I who have done this"—and this spoils everything.

Gurdjieff: I will give you a sacred secret. You remember Beelzebub—there are two currents, two rivers. You have to cross from one to the other; you are like fish whose natural element is water and who are obliged to live in the air. You must now learn to live in both currents at once. There is the habitual current which is ordinary life in which you live, and then in you must exist the other current, the second current, which is your interior life. Up to now you have had contact with yourself only when you were alone, quiet, now you must learn with others. When you are with a person, remain in your own current, in your interior current.

Question: In the system, it seems that satisfactions, pleasures, are rejected? Are they all? Have I understood rightly?

Gurdjieff: All pleasures are merde. All pleasures make you a slave. Your satisfaction. There are two qualities of pleasure; two qualities of agreeable sensations. On one side objective pleasure; if you work well and get a result, you can have satisfaction of yourself. This is good satisfaction which crowns effort. Other, mechanical pleasures destroy you. You are lost in them. They are all injurious, except for giving oneself voluntary relaxation, necessary for an aim.

Question: I notice in myself a dryness, an absence of emotions. I live either in indifference or hostility. What is to be done?

Gurdjieff: You interest me. I wish to help you. Are your parents still alive? We have not known them, but perhaps they had souls. Perhaps they suffered. They cannot do any more where they are, they have no bodies. You must do something for them. You must think of them. You must picture them to yourself, see them again, have their faces before your eyes, you must think of all that you owe them. You are a small piece of them, of their life. You must love them, express your gratitude to them. Think back on all they have done for you. You must see your mistakes towards them. Persist in this, reconstruct the scenes when you made them suffer, perhaps cry. Re-live the times when you were a bad child. You must have remorse of conscience. Remorse. One must suffer voluntarily to repair. One must pay for the past. The past must be repaired. Search in your past. Create remorse. Doctor, you also do this exercise. For the moment, your parents are your God. You cannot know God. He is too far away. There is no place for Him in you. Your parents are God, they are the future place for God in you. You owe them everything, life, everything. Work first with them; after there will be other exercises.

Question: I have done the work which you gave us. Really I love my parents very much and I have discovered a very special quality of emotion; during one second perhaps, one particle of real love, also great suffering, a real suffering for my sins towards them. Of remorse. The two emotions were there at the same time, very vivid suffering and happiness given by the feeling of love. It was the remorse which brought happiness, for after that disappeared the happiness also disappeared. Sometimes when I am attending my patients I have discovered in myself for a second emotions of love of the same quality. And at that moment I could relieve their physical sufferings and bring them a feeling of happiness. Is there a connection?

Gurdjieff: Real love is the basis of all, the foundations, the Source. The religions have perverted and deformed love. It was by love that Jesus performed miracles. Real love joined with magnetism. All accumulated vibrations create a current. This current brings the force of love. Real love is a cosmic force which goes through us. If we crystallise it, it becomes a power—the greatest power in the world. Later you will study magnetism in books, no matter which, it will give you material. And with love as a basis, you will be able to cure paralytics and make the blind see.

Question: I have been surprised by the acuteness of sensations observed for a long time, so intense, so vivid, with all the impressions I had in myself and which came back.

Gurdjieff: This is normal. Our centres register everything, from the hour of one's birth. If I put you into an hypnotic sleep, you can tell me what went on around you a week after your birth. Everything is written, everything is there. A subject put to sleep by me told me the pulse rate of the person who was beside him at the moment which I made him re-live. Everything is written, as on a photograph, but a thousand times more sensitive. That is why you must be careful of the inscriptions. Choose them. (Beelzebub: "Watch the purity of your rolls.")

Question: Does this work bring something to my parents? Does it touch them, give them something?

Gurdjieff: You must do this for yourself, for repairing. Have remorse. Let your remorse be as strong as possible. It is this remorse which counts; it is the suffering which matters; voluntary suffering which pays for the past, which repairs the errors.

Question: I have discovered the same quality of emotions of which we spoke, but it gives me such an interior fullness, such a sensation of happiness that I no longer feel remorse; I grudge myself this happiness, for I have not deserved it.

Gurdjieff: You have imagination and fantasy. I have always said so. You are a representative of art. Fou-fou. There is no weight. It is light. Philosophy, imagination. A state is a result. It is this which gives weight. This is the counter balance of real happiness which goes in step with it. At the same time in order that it should be genuine, one must not have one without the other. Your nature has a tendency (the result of inertia); you let yourself go towards this tendency of having extraordinary states without a real basis, without weight. You must eliminate this, drive it away. As soon as a state of satisfaction arises, make "tchik." Crush it, eliminate it. Work on remorse, remember yourself, revive the scenes when you were a bad child, when you made your parents cry, perhaps. Feel again in all the details, find your faults again. Search in your past. Suffer. In that suffering you can have real happiness given by real love.

There are two different things under different laws: (1) The organic body; (2) the psychic body. The organic body obeys its laws. It only wishes to satisfy its needs—eating, sleeping, sex. It knows nothing else. It wishes nothing else. It is a real animal. One must feel it as an animal. One must feel it as a stranger. One must subdue it, train it and make it obey, instead of obeying it.

The psychic body knows something other than the organic body. It has other needs, other aspirations, other desires. It belongs to a different world, it is of a different nature. There is a conflict between these two bodies—one wishes, the other does not. It is a struggle which one must reinforce voluntarily, by our work, by our will. It is this fight which exists naturally, which is the specific state of man, which we must use to create a third thing, a third state different from the other two, which is the Master, which is united with something else.

The task is therefore something precise which reinforces this struggle, because by struggle and *only* by struggle can a new possibility of being be born. For instance, my organism is in the habit of smoking. That is its need. I do not wish to smoke—I eliminate this habit. The need is always there but I refuse to satisfy it. There is a struggle, a conscious voluntary struggle which calls the third force. It is the third force which will be the factor—"I"—which will conciliate and make the equilibrium.

The body is an animal. The psyche is a child. One must educate the one and the other. Take the body, make it understand that it must obey, not command. Put each one in its place. One must know oneself. One must see what goes on. Take a task which is within your possibility, very small to begin with. On eating. On a habit. Each one knows himself and can find a task; it is his interior thing, a will which is opposed to a need and creates struggle. The only possibility of creating a second body is by an accumulation of a different substance. The only aim is that everything should serve this aim.

Question: I have thoroughly understood all during the week what you told me last week about the physical body and the psychic body and all the week I have worked in this direction; I have struggled. One night I was asleep. I was awakened by my son—I have a four-year-old son—who had been bitten by mosquitoes and who was in pain and began to cry and call for me. He was suffering and crying. I went to him and because he was crying and suffering, before I even had the time to see myself, I beat him. I did not allow myself to go to sleep again. How can I crush this violence in myself? I have seen what my body is, what it is capable of and its reaction after a week of work on it.

Gurdjieff: There are forces around you, foreign to you. It is possible that when a man really works, really wishes to struggle, they produce an event like this. They can even create the mosquitoes. In any case, whether it was this or chance, nothing could have been better. There you have felt, you have understood, not with your head only. I am very glad and I ask you now to make notes of all that happens in your work for a week, two weeks, three weeks, and you will speak about it here, because this will be useful for your companions. And do not forget that now your son is your master. Thank him. For me, he is my friend. And I charge you with a commission for him; five candies a day for a year.

[Mr. Gurdjieff has given an exercise and afterwards he shows the group an engraving representing seven Oriental dancers, with headdresses like gigantic spherical hats surmounted by antennas; they are striking in cadence their tambourines and blowing into pipes like fifes under the direction of their chief who holds in his hand a sort of pennant. Mr. Gurdjieff asks each pupil to give an opinion as to what this picture represents. No one knows. One woman thinks it is a Tibetan dance.]

Gurdjieff: That is it, the scene is in Tibet. It is a unique thing; a divine music that I heard in the mountains of Tibet. And at the same time, there was no music. And yet down in the foothills below one heard music.

[The group goes to the table and dines. After dinner a student speaks to Mr. Gurdjieff.]

Question: Sir, what does that picture represent that you showed us a while ago?

Gurdjieff: I have told you. I was very astonished when I saw that for the first time. It is a ceremony that takes place in Tibet. There in a valley is a place where special ceremonies are held, not for everyone, not for just anybody. They are reserved for a certain category of initiates. One receives there this initiation and I received it. There is simply a smallish, or rather a large house in a valley. Nothing more. It is there that this ceremony is held. One arrives in the foothills and hears the music. But beautiful like that, never. Truly it was celestial music. Well, one heard the music but saw nothing. Everywhere, all around, there were mountains and that was all. How and from where could this music come? How was it possible? There was not a house near by. One could see far off and there was no one to be seen. Who could be playing this music?

You can imagine what an impression it made and how I was astonished. It was only two years afterwards that I knew the secret and that musicians were playing in the mountains. He that walked at the head of the seven musicians you see in this picture held in his hand an instrument that was a kind of radio. Due to it, he hears what goes on in the valley. And he directs. There is no music, only vibrations that are made by the movements of the body. In his hand

107

is a special instrument. A radio. The radio was discovered only twenty years ago and I saw this instrument thirty-five years ago; the radio did not yet exist. You understand; it is with special movements that these vibrations are produced. These vibrations are gathered into the globe that they have on their heads and sent out through the antennas. There is in the valley a thing something like the instrument that the leader has in his hand with which he establishes the contact. This instrument collects everything and the vibrations come forth in the form of music. But there isn't any music, no instrument. It is the totality of their interior experiences which produces the transmitted result.

Question: But they have tambourines and fifes.

Gurdjieff: That helps. It is everything together that gives that, but they don't play music with that. The interesting thing is that the movements and the interior exercises are what give the music. Very interesting thing. What you have all done just a while ago is child's play beside that. And what must be done is much more difficult. But it is well understood that interior experiences can give vibrations and that a strong experience of that kind can give vibrations capable of producing divine music. One can arrive at such results thanks to an exact effort in the work. If everything is not absolutely harmonious, there is cacophony. You must have the exact attitude necessary for this in order to produce celestial music. We have read in a chapter of the Second Series [Meetings with Remarkable Men] about Prince Lubovedsky some details about the temples of Tibet where the priestesses have studied such movements from infancy before the branched instrument which expressed the law of seven. They were able to perform their dances effectively only after years of study. It is the same for these dancers. They have studied these movements from childhood and only when they are old they may participate in the ceremony. You can imagine how they have had to work in order to be specialists.

You see my astonishment? I have seen a thousand astonishing things. But I remember still my stupefaction at this. Afterwards I understood. But during two or three days I could not sleep; I wanted to know. I had heard the music and I hadn't seen anywhere a man or a house or a movement. Nothing but mountains and snow. Nothing more. And I was hearing that music. I was like a madman. Afterwards, in studying this, I quieted myself and learned what it was about. But you understand now why I repeat always among other things—do not, for example, make a movement with the leg which should be made only with the foot. Perhaps you will need that leg for something else. You must do everything exactly from the beginning. But you must respect each detail. We will not play music. It isn't a question of music but a real feeling of the "I am." There are seven exercises for that. This present exercise is one of them. You can repeat for a thousand years "I am" with your mind; it will give you nothing real. This exercise can, however. That is why you must do it with exactitude from the beginning. Only an exactness in your work can give exact results. It's like what I heard in those mountains. One movement not exactly executed among seven persons and the result would be a cacophony. Everything depends on the totality.

And our Mr. District Attorney writes and writes. How can he understand all this when I myself do not very well understand all that I have been saying.

*[The second part of exercise one is described to some pupils and
some new people are questioned and advised.]*

Gurdjieff: Little one, what is your question?

Luc: The exercise which consists in demanding of the body the
substances necessary to bring to the face expressions of goodness,
justice, honesty, impartiality and intelligence has led me to recon-
sider each of these terms and particularly honesty. What is the
relation of honesty, the balance between what one takes and what
one gives in return? I had more satisfaction when I was earning less
and am embarrassed now in a more comfortable and easy situation—

Gurdjieff: I have already understood your question. Go on.

Luc: I feel doubtful about my honesty, even though I give away
three-quarters of my money. I want my life founded on such
principles that my means of livelihood could be purified.

Gurdjieff: And now, will you formulate your question?

Luc: By what can one feel that one is honest?

Gurdjieff: There is a principle, a criterion: when you have given
yourself your word to do something and you have done it, you have
a certain feeling of contentment. It is this feeling of satisfaction in
yourself which shows you that you are honest. You understand this
feeling?

Luc: Yes. But now in my everyday life I have more and more to use
tricks and that revolts me.

Gurdjieff: That is exterior life. You do this for them. I have already
said now you must be an absolute egoist, a good egoist. For the sake
of future altruism. Today you cannot give much to others, and if you
try to, you will not be able to change yourself, you will remain what
you are. You must make the sacrifice of giving to another. But you
must give yourself your word that you will make it up to him in
future ten-fold. So you compromise. You have two clues, two
principles; satisfaction in yourself and promise to pay back much
more later on. Outwardly, one plays one's role, according to what
the situation demands, and inwardly one does not identify. If you
are working inwardly, nature will help you. For the man who is

working, nature is a sister of charity; she brings him what he has need of for his work. If you need money for your work, even if you do nothing to get it, the money will come to you from all sides. In another case, nature will cut off all a man's resources if it is necessary for his work. *[To Simone]* Do you understand? For instance, had you had money a certain evening, you would have gone to a café but having none, you stayed at home and worked. Nature is more intelligent than you; she knows better than you which are the best conditions for your work; and if you work, nature calls on conscious spirits who will arrange for you the conditions you need. For ordinary man, for the man who does not work, there is nothing but chance. But for the man who works, nature gives him through conscious spirits all that he needs.

Philippe: What you have just said has given me more than all the exercises. I feel in myself at this moment what spirit is. I feel a life in me. Now I understand what I must do. I must give up my "scale." I must undertake obligations, give myself my word concerning small things, not big ones which are too far from me.

Gurdjieff: There is a law which is formulated very simply. A man must keep his given word; in all cases, whatever happens. It is an absolute command. If you have given your word to come and see me at a certain time, even if they cut you in pieces, kill you, you must come. A small thing but perhaps it is connected with many others which you do not know. If you do not come, it may cost a million francs. It will upset the appointment I have after yours and that will make it necessary to change something else and so on through a chain of events you cannot foresee. If one small thing is not carried out, then no big thing will be carried out. With big things it is easy; they are far away and you are only concerned with them from time to time, when it pleases you. But small things are near you all the time, whether you want it or not. Try once to give yourself your word about a small thing. Not about everything, because a promise given must be held to and you must know that you are capable of keeping it. Take a small thing that you can do.

[After luncheon Mr. Gurdjieff reproached "T." for not fulfilling well his duties, his obligations as director.]

Gurdjieff: It is a small thing, but if one understands how one must direct one's affairs in life, it is a big thing. There is not one aspect,

111

there are seven. If you have seven affairs and you do one well, the six others can even go well automatically. You neglect one, even though for the first time in your life, the result is bad. For instance, if you undertake the obligation of directing the serving, you must direct all the details. Forget everything, even your God, to supervise all details with exactitude. If you are director, nothing exists but that, even if you have affairs worth millions. Those you must forget. Do well that which you have to do. When your affairs worth millions come up, you will do them the same way. Do not see just one aspect but seven and all will be well. If one aspect is not good, nothing is good. Accustom yourself to do well all things at the time, and parallel with this, you will learn to do everything well. You are here. You sacrifice everything else. All your presence, all your thought, all your associations must be drawn to the affair which constitutes your work. If you do well what you have to do in the w.c., you will also do well that which you have to do in church. If you do not do well what you have to do in the w.c., you will not do anything well in church either. In the ordinary things of life you must fulfil all your obligations, even think about them two or three weeks ahead and never fail. You have the time. Think of everything, prepare everything. You are always losing time. With such an interior organisation, a man will never go far.

Question: Can I ask a question?

Gurdjieff: Why do you make a fly from an elephant? If you have a question, ask it. It is my speciality to talk, talk, talk. Help me to stop my machine from talking. Ask your question.

[He asks about his search for God, his doubts and struggles.]

Gurdjieff: I have already answered this question when someone asked the same thing. I said: if you do not have an ideal, if you do not believe in God, then your father, your mother, your teacher can serve for you as an ideal.

Question: I have an ideal, I have always been a Catholic. But I no longer see Jesus Christ in the same way.

Gurdjieff: In the beginning Catholicism was very good, but not latterly. They searched for midday at two o'clock; they diluted everything. In the beginning it was superior to the Orthodox religion and to all others.

Question: I cannot recapture the faith of my childhood.

Gurdjieff: That is not necessary. You have lost that possibility. You are no longer a child, you are big now. You should have logic and not search automatically. To have direct contact with God is impossible. Millions and millions of nonentities wish to have relations with Mr. God direct. This is impossible. But you can have a relation in this line. What you do here, for instance, has this changed your interior ideal—since you took part in our conversations? [Yes] Then perhaps you have confidence in the person who directs here? [Yes] Then he can serve as teacher in the meantime.

Question: That does not satisfy me entirely. I want something else.

Gurdjieff: Then make a programme. You do not know what you want. I wish you to understand that your nearest—father, mother, teacher—can serve as your ideal in place of God. The real God, forget Him. As you are, you can never have relations with God. When you have grown, this could be, but you are one among millions of nonentities. Meantime, take as an ideal whoever is nearest and then you can pray to God, because this person has an ideal also, this ideal has in turn an ideal and so on, on to God. God is far, there are many stages before you reach Him, do not think about Him. Your ideal will be your God. Later you can have another ideal.

Mme de Salzmann: God is much too far away. You are too small to have direct contact with Him. Only he who is immediately above you can be God for you. He is a God who in his turn has a God. It is a ladder, there is always something above. Each degree [rung] leads you to another and you get your answer by the same chain.

Gurdjieff: You cannot pray directly to God. You imagine so, but you waste your time. It is from there that psychopathy comes. Like a monk. He says directly, "God." He manipulates like this *[gestures]* and sixty years later he perishes like a dog without ever having received anything. He wanted God directly. No one has seen Him, for the law of contacts is strict. This law exists everywhere. You will look for your God when you have felt yourself guided in the right direction, on a good road, for instance by Mme de Salzmann. Then she will be your God. She is not God, but she will be your first stage; you can have contact with God through her; make all your prayers and good manifestations pass through her and that itself will make

113

contact with the next stage. Then a third stage and finally it is possible that your prayer will reach the real God. Exactly like the telegraph; a message to a relative in the country near Lyons. First from Paris to Lyons; then to another town, then to the village, then to your relative's house. By stages and it takes some time.

[A question about "injustices."]

Gurdjieff: You know "Justice" is a big word—it is a big thing in the world. Objective things are not small things like microbes, they go according to law, as the law has accustomed them to go. Remember; as you sow, so you will reap. Not only people reap, but also families and nations. It often happens that that which happens on earth comes from something which was done by a father or a grandfather. The results converge on you, the son or grandson, it is you who have to regulate them. This is not an injustice, it is a very great honour for you; it will be a means which will allow you to regulate the past of your father, grandfather, great-grandfather. If misfortunes come to you in your youth, it means that someone brought them—for this you must reap. He is dead, it is another on earth who reaps. You must not look at yourself egoistically. You are a link in the chain of your blood. Be proud of it, it is an honour to be this link. The more you are obliged to repair the past, the more you will have remorse of conscience. You will succeed in remembering all that which you have not done as you should in the past. Those things which you have done contrary to *Justice* have mortified your grandfather. Thus you can have ten times more remorse of conscience and your worth will augment in proportion.

You are not tail of a donkey. You have responsibilities, a family. All your family, past and future, depend on you. Your entire family depends on the way you repair the past. If you repair for everyone, it is good. If you do not repair for everyone, it is bad. You see your situation. Logically, do you see what Justice is? Justice is not occupied with your little affairs, unredeemed pledges, it is occupied with big things. It is idiotic to believe God thinks of small things. It is the same with Justice. Justice does not touch all that, and at the same time, nothing is done on earth without it. Search for the reasons. You are obliged to have a position of responsibility in the line of your blood; you must work more to repair the past. It is difficult to understand all at once.

[A man asserts he cannot work well, can do nothing to his satisfaction, is troubled by conscience.]

Gurdjieff: It is impossible to do this all at once, one must search. Begin with a small thing. When you wake, remember consciously to put on the left sock first, instead of the right one, remembering yourself. Wash the left ear first, not the one you are in habit of washing. Make a programme. Always either a fly or something else will appear to prevent you from carrying out this programme. But even if there is a fire, do what I tell you. Then when you go out into the street, instead of looking into the window on the left at the blonde who interests you, look towards the window on the right at the brunette. And so on. If you do not succeed in trying this, do not speak of it any more. If you do this, you can ask your question again, and I will reply and explain a thousand more details.

Question: At the bottom of all my negative emotions there are two things; on one side, the opinion I have of myself, on the other a certain fear. If I succeed in remembering my nothingness, the opinion of myself changes and no longer hinders me, but the fear grows and determines the negative emotion and prevents me from resisting, I have not found a means of struggling against this fear.

Gurdjieff: One must decide: "All or nothing." It is simple, all or nothing. If you know your past nothingness, then decide; either you want to transfer this nothingness into something, or you will perish. If you decide, all or nothing, after this your fear will be less important. If you decide to perish, then that is another question. You are not frightened? [No] Then the fear is nothing. This is the means of liquidating your fear. What you first said about your opinion of yourself is fou-fou. Your father was already fou-fou. So what opinion can you have? You are a nonentity, merde. You must understand this. Objectively what opinion can you have? You can do nothing. It is all imagination. You cannot even make a cigarette. You must decide within the field of your nothingness. The all or nothing can end your fear. Either something will happen or you will perish like a dog. You should not exist as you are. You are a source of evil in the world, for your nearest and for everyone. Either you will cease to be such a source in order to acquire a real individuality, real not fantasy, or—perish. Have you understood? It is a new "Justice," it has another dress. A belt and a hat also—a tall hat.

Mme Dubeau: It is difficult for me to separate what I sense, what is true, from what is imaginary; difficult to see if what I sense has a real basis. For example, it seems impossible in the exercise to fill my arms . . .

Gurdjieff: I told you to expect nothing from this exercise. It is the exercise which will give you understanding. Others will come after. Then perhaps you will find it possible to understand what is fantasy and what is real. To understand, it is necessary to *do*, to have experience. The exercises will give you experience. These exercises were established centuries ago, even before Europe existed.

Pomereu: I would like to know whether the work is compatible with ambition—a desire for power—in the external world.

Gurdjieff: If it helps you with your exercise, you can do it. For example, you can even kill someone. I have given you this categorical advice: Be an egoist. You can do nothing at present. First put yourself solidly on your feet. After that, you can do something. Your question is abstract.

Pomereu: Can one have ambition outside the work?

Gurdjieff: You can give it to yourself as a task but you mustn't count on succeeding—you may or may not. It may perhaps be compatible with the work.

Pomereu: So it is not necessary to try and destroy it right away?

Gurdjieff: No. But if it upsets your serious work, if it is a weakness, you must kill it. If you can do it consciously, you can keep it.

P: But if it is a physical thing . . .

Gurdjieff: It can be a physical thing, but not automatic. Give yourself a conscious task and carry it out, even by inertia.

P: How can I know that my decision is conscious? If I want money, for instance, it is surely from cupidity.

Gurdjieff: Another question. What you have acquired through the work must not be used in ordinary life. So long as you have to do with me, you must outwardly play a role, but inwardly you must learn never to identify. During the work such things do come— extraordinary possibilities—you must never use them for ordinary life.

Mlle Dollinger: Can one be helped in work by prayer and how can one pray?

Gurdjieff: You can only pray with your three centres, and at the same time it is an exercise. What interests me is not your prayer, it is your concentration with your three centres. Your prayer goes no farther than your atmosphere [aura]. When your prayer can go as far as America, you will be able to pray to the President.

Mlle D: How can one pray with the three centres?

Gurdjieff: Now you must do a serious thing. Learn, for the sake of the future, to concentrate not only with one centre but with the three. You must think, feel and sense. This is important. For this there are different exercises. You can pray, sing—anything you like— but with the three centres.

Hignette: The rule formulated just now leaves me wondering. It seems to me that sometimes one can't help using certain results of work. I am thinking of my class and how differently I manage it now from before.

Gurdjieff: What I wish to tell you is something different. We were not speaking of that. This is a natural thing. You could even have done that without me. Each year you are older, more practiced. You gain experience and change your way of going about things.

Alain: Sometimes I succeed in reaching a kind of thinking which is clearer and bigger, in which I understand many more things. Can I use this?

Gurdjieff: Just do your exercises . . . Exactly as one learns to play the piano. First of all, you do many exercises before playing a tune. Now you must do your exercise and live as before. No one must notice that you are inwardly working. That is your aim—inwardly not to identify. To play a role is not an aim, but a means.

A: I wanted more definite directions how not to identify.

Gurdjieff: Everything comes in its time, only necessary practise. You are philosophising. Now your aim is not to identify. Consider your past actions. What can you say of them impartially? This will serve as a clue for your work and you will recognise that you were always identified. It is necessary for us to be inwardly impartial. This is impossible for the moment. We look at each thing, animate or inanimate, partially. This is where our weakness lies.

Horande: Sir, I am in a bad way at the moment and I am very tired.

Gurdjieff: I told you from the start, doctor, this work burns a lot of electricity.

H: For a week I haven't been able to do my exercise, even the simple effort to remember for a quarter of an hour, because I have been intoxicated by the results I have had. I think about work, but I don't succeed in doing anything definite.

Gurdjieff: You cannot expect result yet. You can only do the exercises. To be able to play tunes takes a long time. Perhaps you had an illusion, then a disillusionment. It comes like that. Think only of the future, when your playing may acquire a different quality and you may become a pianist.

Mme D: My way of reasoning sometimes makes me think that all this is a dream. When I don't feel like working, I tell myself all this isn't true.

Gurdjieff: You have many dogs in you. As "Mr. Gurdjieff" I cannot help you, but only as a doctor. But I have not the right to practise in France. I take on only English and American patients.

Mme D: Then I might as well give up.

Gurdjieff: You must get over this crisis. Now if you have recognised your nothingness, you can make a real decision to change something. If I had a pill to calm you, I wouldn't give it to you. You must thank nature that this crisis has begun, and that it has begun so soon. Philippe has a crisis like that twice a year.

Denise: Is sincerity compatible with spontaneity?

Gurdjieff: They can go together, but it is desirable that they don't go together. Spontaneity is not controlled. You must not be sincere with others, but with yourself. You must trust no one, neither sister nor brother. You must be sincere with yourself. If you are sincere with another, you put all your cards on the table. He will sit on your head. This sincerity is a disease. Perhaps you have nothing inside, but the other imagines that you have something. Let him imagine it.

Aboulker: You advised me to make a break in my work this week. This break has shown me that I was working just enough to keep me satisfied and subdue my negative emotions. When I do not work, I have a feeling of remorse; negative emotions take up the whole of me. For instance, I am seized constantly by envy of others.

Gurdjieff: It is not your fault. It is the fault of your mother and father. We will destroy the results of this upbringing.

Lanctin: I have noticed that when I work, at the same time certain coarse tendencies and desires, certain appetites for low things become stronger and take a more important place than before.

Gurdjieff: In this room there are twelve people. If you wanted to bring in two more people, it would be necessary for two of the people already here to go out. It is the same for you. Room has to be made and in order to make room, whatever occupies this room has to go out. If one person wants to go out while another wishes to come in, they are stopped, one by the other. They have their eye on the door. Perhaps you are in that situation. In this work there must be no compromise. Little by little you make room. One person goes out, another comes in.

Lacaze: Monsieur Gurdjieff—

Gurdjieff: It is a long time now since I was Gurdjieff.

L: This week there came to me, quite apart from the exercises and work, a certain taste of myself which I have never felt till now, and which forces me to be in a part of myself that usually I am never in. This taste is dissipated because I don't know what to do with it; I don't want it to be lost but help me go further.

Gurdjieff: You must stop all things and do inwardly what has to be done for your work and what can help you for your future.

L: But this feeling comes at a moment when I am doing something quite different, when I am busy with people and can't stop what I am doing.

Gurdjieff: We are not speaking about things in life. This is something quite different. You must play a role. For instance, you shake hands with the right hand. You don't need to think for that.

Zuber: I found myself this week in a situation where I should have felt remorse but in fact I felt only a slight twinge which couldn't be compared to the real feeling. I would like to know whether there are some special means for experiencing remorse.

Gurdjieff: Think of all you have done in your life, all moments when you haven't been as you should have been. You remember and at the same time you have a feeling of remorse.

Solange: I have noticed that I used to have stronger feelings of remorse than now that I am working. I had violent feelings; now they are intellectual. I judge my actions but I don't feel as I used to feel.

Gurdjieff: It is quite a simple thing. Before you used to make elephant from fly and fly from elephant. That is the way you are by nature. Now you see fly as a fly and elephant as an elephant.

S: I am wondering if I should keep on with the work I am doing or take up something else better suited to my capacities. I should like to have an aim in life.

Gurdjieff: My advice is do something quite new, without any connection with what you are doing at present. The less you are satisfied with your work, the greater your possibility of doing more. Start again to learn for the future. A new career is the very best thing for you. In life one can make all sorts of compromises, but with this work there are none. You must change your whole outer life and begin all over again.

Gilles: I have little knowledge of myself, especially of my essence. I never know how to be certain about myself. What means of investigation can I use to know if a thing comes from me or not?

Gurdjieff: Now you are philosophising. Necessary begin from something real. Now this is empty for me because you are empty. You did not start on the way of a real man. This is education. Seven factors were absent from your upbringing. I can tell you the first. You were not taught that for you your father is your God. For each man, up to a certain age, his father must be his God. God loves him who esteems his father. When the father dies, then there is a place where God can enter in. You have not this relationship with your father and your question springs from that. Now take as a task to put down all these factors in yourself which hinder you; establish a real relationship with your father.

Mme Dubeau: But if the father is unworthy—low?

Gurdjieff: Even if he is the worst criminal, if he is merde, the lowest among men, you must recognise your obligation. You don't know why he has become like that. Here is a law. He created you. You owe your existence to him. And he is answerable for your life in another world. If he is the lowest of men in the eyes of everyone, let it be so—but inwardly you must feel your obligation. You have to pay him for your existence.

Gilles: But in order to establish a right relationship with someone, one has to be sure of what one is oneself.

Gurdjieff: You divide yourself in two parts. Inwardly you must not identify, outwardly you must play a role. Take all things as your guide. Your task now is to acquire inner freedom. This is the starting point for going further. And for that you have to do what I have told you. What does it mean, to play a role? Try to understand it in a broader sense. Do everything that gives him pleasure. If he likes you to sit on his right, sit on his right. If at another moment he prefers the opposite, do it. Subjective role. With each person a different role. You accustom yourself to fulfil obligations. It is one of the aspects of the future of a free man. Not necessary to philosophise. After, yes. First prepare the ground. The ground has seven aspects.

After that, you can go as you like. In future, with each man you must play a role; for your egoism. To make each person your slave. You do not do what you like, but what he likes.

Mme D: Towards one's father, is it an inner or outer obligation?

Gurdjieff: I said that inwardly you have objective obligations. But at the same time you play a role with him outwardly, as with everyone. This is difficult at the beginning, but later you will come to see how everything changes. Perhaps later your father will become your slave; even God can become your slave.

Denise: So at present we should not do what we like.

Gurdjieff: You have no time now to satisfy your weakness. You must kill it. If you work, you must not temporise with your weakness. You must be merciless.

Denise: Even if the object is to comfort someone else?

Gurdjieff: We are speaking of ourselves at this moment.

Denise: For instance, I am living among people who talk always of devotion and mutual help. It used to be my aim too. Now I realise one can do little for others.

Gurdjieff: That is true, it is a fantastic idea. Before, you couldn't do anything good for anybody. Now you give your word to do nothing except for yourself; put yourself on your feet, prepare your future.

D: Now people consider me indifferent.

Gurdjieff: Then you haven't played a role. Otherwise they wouldn't have noticed the change. You are open. Other people must not see what goes on inside you.

D: These are the people who are always around me.

Gurdjieff: It is exactly with such people—

D: It is difficult.

Gurdjieff: Bad things are easy.

Mme D: When I confide to someone something that has happened to me, I feel that what I say loses its force for me. I feel I affect others in getting bad things off my chest.

Gurdjieff: Then you play your role badly.

Mme D: Yes, but it takes the strength from what is bad in me.

Gurdjieff: Today you must sacrifice everything for the sake of the future. All present pleasures. One cannot enter the kingdom of heaven and at the same time eat cakes. Establish good relations with everybody and learn never to identify. This will be a good instrument for changing yourself. At the same time this will create in you a certain energy which will allow you to work better. Things which are easy never give energy.

Pomereu: I would like to know if there is a better way to use physical energy than doing sports.

Gurdjieff: Exercise with numbers, names and so on. To do it well one must have five times as much energy as you have.

P: But we haven't done them yet.

Gurdjieff: Well, do the one which was given on Sunday. In one-half hour I can pump into you ten times more energy than you have. If you feel as you say, it shows you haven't understood.

Mme D: For a long time I didn't work because I felt I wasn't doing the exercise of filling the body rightly. Then I started again.

Gurdjieff: Go on trying. It comes little by little. Ten times it may not come, but the eleventh time—you have to do and do all the exercises. First you have to get a taste for them, and then it becomes easy. Follow the rules carefully; relax yourself, and so on, and that will help you. Sooner or later you will succeed. But one must not spare oneself.

D: I haven't really the feeling of filling the body, but a general feeling.

Gurdjieff: At the beginning you can use that.

Gerbeau: Can one have a more subtle knowledge of one's essence? My sensations mingle with a sort of imagination and with very different sensations, often completely opposite. How can I manage to do this better?

Gurdjieff: You have an exercise.

Gb: I don't succeed in doing it at all well.

Gurdjieff: Perhaps because you are thinking of other things; philosophy, fantasy—you have not any essence yet. You are a little dog—a little bit of dog's merde.

Gb: It is because my attention is naturally drawn to very subtle things.

Gurdjieff: Stick to two times two are four. You go too far ahead. Hence these misunderstandings.

A: Yet in lots of ways I remain on one spot.

Gurdjieff: Because you go on ahead. (Marvellous.)

A: In connection with Sunday's exercise, I wonder if it isn't a question of sex which prevents me from doing it well?

Gurdjieff: Don't philosophise. For you specially, I give an exercise. Each time you feel the beginning of weakness, relax and then think seriously: "I wish the result of my weakness to become my own strength." This will accumulate in you for your future work. Each man knows which weakness he has in him. Each time this weakness appears in you, stop yourself and do this exercise. It is a very necessary exercise for you. You will talk about it sincerely one day with Mme de Salzmann.

Horande: I have a little girl, four years old. What role should I play with her?

Gurdjieff: Role of father.

H: But I feel I am not a real father.

Gurdjieff: Be a good father. Do not encourage, criticise everything, so that the child shall not have imagination. But inwardly, one loves the child. In this way your real love will come into being.

H: There are moments when I feel that it is necessary to be severe. At other times I let my affection show through.

Gurdjieff: It must not show. It must be just. If once you show your affection, your authority will be crippled. You must never show a child your inner self. Your weakness—to love, to caress, and so on—leave that to everyone else. Not you. A father's authority is a very important thing. And in this way you will be a real father.

Hignette: Isn't there a risk of making the child timid and stifling its personality?

Gurdjieff: If he does as I have explained, the child will not be afraid. He will have respect. It is another quality of fear. You must not frighten him.

Aboulker: I have tried to feel remorse of conscience, but the remorse overwhelms me. I cannot forget that it was from remorse that Judas hanged himself.

Gurdjieff: Why do you speak of Judas in this case? What do you know of Judas? He was a great initiate. He was the second disciple after St. John the Baptist. All that is told about him is false. If you wish to know, he was even the master of Christ.

Aboulker: The search for remorse leads me to depression. I must be doing the exercise wrongly. How should I try to find remorse?

Gurdjieff: In order to experience remorse it is necessary to awaken real will to remember real aim. You must destroy tranquillity.

Dr. A: I have felt remorse in flashes two or three times. But I do not know how to make it come. When I look for it intentionally, I do not recapture this quality but find the kind that depresses me.

Gurdjieff: When remorse comes without self-love, it gives us the desire for something better. But when it is mixed with self-love, it weighs you down. The effect of true remorse is hatred of yourself, repugnance towards yourself. These two things make up true remorse of conscience.

Dr. A: One time when I felt it I was nauseated, literally.

Gurdjieff: You have to feel a lot of that in order to kill your enemy. When you feel this depression you should do the "I am," then you needn't be afraid of becoming more depressed. Only through this impulse can you transcend your nothingness. You should rejoice that an impulse has awakened in you a real will to change. You must not stand on ceremony with self-love. Self-love is your greatest enemy. One must punish oneself mercilessly against this filthy creature. Not only you—but everybody. The feeling of remorse can make reparation for all things all the mistakes of our parents, of your educators, your childhood companions. You must acquire the inner freedom which will make you worthy to become a candidate for future man. My dear doctor, this is what I advise and it is a very difficult thing. It is not pleasant, but that is not my fault. If you wish to have a future, try this in the present. The more you experience it, the more possibility you have for the future. You must succeed in bringing remorse of conscience to a point where it becomes hatred of self and hatred of your past, of your parents, of the upbringing you have had. Curse everything. Call upon your ideal to help you to bear the burden and to become worthy of it. On one hand you curse your past; on the other, in the name of your future, you give your word—as against this curse—to help them [parents] as much as you can. You must reach the point where conscience speaks mercilessly in you.

Mme Etievan: I have experienced the same depression as the doctor, but I no longer have it. I find myself as I was before.

Gurdjieff: I am suspicious of something; perhaps you are getting used to it automatically. That is also bad—an idée fixe. One cannot become accustomed to remorse; it must penetrate to the inner self. If you become accustomed, you make it automatic; it becomes external, without weight, you do it with your head only. You are wasting your time. Begin again more mercilessly. You must do this with the three centres, not only with your head.

Kahn: When I examine the few years I have been in the work, I notice I have never lacked driving force, but that part of me has always run away from work. I saw this when you told me I lacked physical will. Where can I get the force which will give me physical will?

Gurdjieff: Only one thing can help you. You must suffer physically. For instance, don't eat enough; be hungry. Or, if your organism doesn't like cold water, make yourself bear cold water. Same with hot water. Do the opposite of what your body is in the habit of doing. Make it suffer. It is the one and only way to make the force you lack. Not a mental suffering. We have seven kinds of suffering. For you, bodily suffering is necessary. With your mind you can mercilessly govern your body, make it suffer. In you, two parts work, but the body does not. Have you understood your emotion? If you have observed it, if you believe me, do this, struggle, suffer. Afterwards you will be able to work on yourself. I am glad you came to this question by yourself.

Mme D: I cannot master the exercise. I get identified. When I am quiet I succeed better.

Gurdjieff: Then it is less useful.

Mme D: Another difficulty. When I visualise a dead person, I have no contact with him. I even have the impression of never having seen him.

Gurdjieff: Very good example for you. Perhaps you only know that person with one part of yourself—the intellectual part, for instance—and now you wish to change and picture them with feeling. You will have contact with all your centres, but one by one.

Mme D: I must find someone who fulfils the conditions.

Gurdjieff: Perhaps you will never find such a person. Perhaps you are one-sided. If you cannot find one person, take two or three. With one you will be in the feeling part, with another in thinking and so on.

Pomereu: I have noticed that when I watch my breathing I am better able to remember myself. Should I do this?

Gurdjieff: Not if you think there is risk of it becoming a fixed idea. If it helps you, continue. Only you can judge.

P: How would I know that it is a fixed idea?

Gurdjieff: Now I have understood. By your question. I have understood your inner state. What is the centre of gravity of your work?

P: The exercise which consists of feeding the "I" and the seven breaths.

Gurdjieff: Which is the one that interests you most, gives you most confidence?

P: I don't do them in the same conditions. Both are important for me.

Gurdjieff: Change the conditions in which you do the exercises. Do the one which you have been doing in the time set aside for working, in life, and vice versa. Change the time to overcome automatism. I am suspicious of something and this may make it clear to me.

[Mme Vera Daumal asks a question about the exercise of seven breaths.]

Mme Vera Daumal: Is this the right way to continue or must I clean up more?

Gurdjieff: Continue. Perhaps you are doing it with only part of yourself. Now you begin to awake, that produces a misunderstanding. Go on until you have objective contact with your three centres. Contact with one is only hysteria. A real person is himself. I am me; if I love, it is with the whole of my being; if I hate also.

V.D: I don't want any more of that.

Gurdjieff: Then do it all the time, fix a new habit. After that I will help you.

V.D: I have made a great effort all week. I have felt something new.

Gurdjieff: For the first time something has awakened in you. But you are not used to it yet, you haven't yet enough material. You are on the right road. If you are able to curse and be disgusted by your past, that will help you. Realise how much time you have lost. That is remorse of conscience. In this way you prepare a good future. Without bad things, good things never come.

Wack: There is one part of me that I never succeed in bringing up intentionally when I try to remember myself. This part only awakes as a result of an outside shock. How can I make it appear?

Gurdjieff: You must kill something in yourself. You have to make room for this new feeling. We have in our system a definite number of factors. In you all the factors are already written upon, like gramophone records, and these inscriptions are already false. You must destroy one of these records, put another in its place.

W: How can one destroy it?

Gurdjieff: By a definite force. Choose an external ideal. Religious faith, for instance. Something which you are sure about and which is outside yourself. Then liquidate this belief, destroy it. You will lose nothing, for it is false. Sooner or later everything must be new in you. For the moment everything is merde. Make room, so as to crystallise a new factor or a new life. I advised you to take faith; perhaps you have another feeling of which you are sure. In any case, there is one which you must succeed in destroying and replacing, so that you will have a real contact with feeling.

W: What will the new factor be?

Gurdjieff: Conscience. Until now you have only crystallised abnormalities coming from the outside.

Mme David: What must one do to follow the advice you give in your book; to persuade all the matters, all the unconscious parts of one's presence, to work as if they were conscious, and so on?

Gurdjieff: It is not my book, it is Mr. Beelzebub's, and it is advice which he is giving to his grandson.

Mme D: Then it is only for his grandson?

Gurdjieff: Beelzebub will explain it to you. As for me, I give you another piece of advice: get accustomed to calling Beelzebub, "my dear grandfather." That will help you. The condition is that you address him respectfully, "my dear grandfather," with all the details. Then perhaps he will answer.

Who has a question to ask about work?

Mme Dubeau: I would like to ask a question about the exercise of the seven breaths. It is an exercise to be done in life. Now I can't even count correctly when I do it in the subway or when I am walking. I have never managed to finish it. I am absorbed inwardly watching this exercise, and can no longer see it as a whole.

Gurdjieff: It is very important. Perhaps you have a fixed idea and it is that which stops you. You must fight as I have advised you.

Mme Dubeau: I cannot master the exercise. I get identified.

Gurdjieff: You must divide this exercise in three separate parts and do one part for three days, another for three days, and then try them all together.

Mme Dubeau: When I am quiet I succeed better.

Gurdjieff: Then it is less useful.

Mme Dubeau: I come up against another difficulty. When I visualise a dead person, I have no contact with them. Sometimes I have the impression that I have never seen them.

Gurdjieff: Very good example for you. Perhaps you only know that person with one part of yourself. The intellectual part, for instance, and now you wish to change and picture them with feeling. You will have contact with all your centres, but one by one.

Mme Dubeau: I must find someone who fulfils the conditions.

Gurdjieff: Perhaps you will never find such a person. Perhaps you are one-sided. If you cannot find one person, take two or three. With one you will be in feeling part, with another in thinking, and so on.

Pomereu: I have noticed that when I watch my breathing I am better able to remember myself. Should I do this?

Gurdjieff: If you think there is any risk of it becoming a fixed idea, do not do it. If you think that that can help you, continue. Only you can judge.

Boby: How would I know that it is a fixed idea?

Gurdjieff: Now I have understood. If you had not asked that question, I would not have understood. I have understood your inner

---

* A continuation of the previous meeting containing some repeated dialogue.

state. What is the centre of gravity of your work?

Boby: The exercise which consists in feeding the "I" and the seven breaths.

Gurdjieff: Which is the one which interests you most, which gives you most confidence?

Boby: I don't do them in the same conditions. Both are important for me.

Gurdjieff: Change the conditions in which you do the exercises. Do the one which you have been doing in your time for working, in life, and vice versa. Change the time. I am afraid of your making the time at which you do it automatic, that you are getting into a habit, and that that will become a fixed idea. By changing the hour, perhaps you can escape the fixed idea and get result. I am suspicious of something and this may make it clear to me. Have you understood?

Boby: Very well.

Hignette: I have a class in which I am able to follow the pupils fairly individually. Some of them practise onanism. How can I tell them strongly not to continue?

Gurdjieff: There are many books in which this affliction is explained. Find these books and read them to them. You can get them together out of class and tell them that whoever lets himself do this will never be a real man, nor a real husband. Read to them, and advise them to give it serious thought. Suggest and prove to them how harmful it is. If there are some who are already in the habit of it, who cannot be convinced, who can no longer be stopped, send them to me, and in two weeks I will get them over it—provided they have a fat cheque-book.

Mlle Dollinger: I do the exercises too much with my head. Often I simply have to stop and go off to the country where I get sensations which give me some balance in myself. After that I find it difficult to take up work again, because it is hard to hold on to these two kinds of life at the same time.

Gurdjieff: How do you know that you have this need?

Mlle Dollinger: When I pass it over, I don't feel balanced.

Gurdjieff: I can't advise you on this question. You need right conditions. The country is not necessary, all you need is a fat cheque-book and a good husband—not a husband like Hignette's pupils. Then everything will go swimmingly. For the moment divide your time.

Mme Daumal: Quite recently I did the exercise of the seven breaths in the way you advised me. This brought me to a moment of self-remembering of a quality that I had never known before. At the same time I experienced a loathing of all contacts through sensation and feeling. I felt at that moment that I didn't want to live with that any longer, but to kill it.

Gurdjieff: Kill what?

Mme Daumal: I saw that someone else's suffering makes me suffer by association. So I tried really to feel "I am" at the same time. Outwardly I was doing what had to be done. Is this the right way to continue or must I clean up still more?

Gurdjieff: Continue. Perhaps you are only doing it with a part of yourself. Now you begin to awake, that produces a misunderstanding. Go on until you have an objective contact with your three centres. Contact with one only is hysteria. A real person is himself. I am me; if I love, it is with the whole of my being, if I hate also.

Mme Daumal: I don't want any more of that.

Gurdjieff: Then do it all the time, fix a new habit. After that, I will help you.

Mme Daumal: I have made a great effort all week. I have felt something new.

Gurdjieff: For the first time something has awakened in you. But you are not used to it yet, you haven't yet enough material. You are on the right road. If you are able to curse and be disgusted by your past, that will help you. See how much time you have lost. This is remorse of conscience. In this way you prepare a good future. Without bad things, good things never come.

Wack: There is one part of me which I never succeed in bringing up intentionally when I try to remember myself. This part only awakes as a result of an outside shock. How can I make it appear?

Gurdjieff: You must kill something in yourself. You have to make room for this new feeling. In our system we have a definite number of factors. In you all the factors are already inscribed like on gramophone records and these inscriptions are already false. You have to destroy one of these records to put another in its place.

Wack: How can one destroy it?

132

Gurdjieff: By a definite force. Choose an external ideal: religious faith, for instance. Something which you are sure about and which is outside yourself. Then liquidate this belief, destroy it. You will lose nothing, for it is false. Sooner or later everything must be new in you. For the moment, everything is merde. Make room, so as to crystallise a new factor for a new life. I advised you to take faith; perhaps you have another feeling of which you are sure. In any case, there is one which you must succeed in destroying and replacing, so that you may have a real contact with feeling.

Wack: What will the new factor be?

Gurdjieff: Conscience. Up till now, you have only crystallised abnormalities coming from outside.

Mme David: What must one do to follow the advice that you give in your book: to persuade all the matters, all the unconscious parts of one's presence, to work as if they were conscious, and so on . . .

Gurdjieff: It is not my book, it is Mr. Beelzebub's, and it is advice which he is giving his grandson.

Mme David: Then it is only for his grandson?

Gurdjieff: Beelzebub will explain it to you. As for me, I give you another piece of advice: get accustomed to calling Beelzebub: "my dear grandfather." That will help you. The condition is that you address him respectfully, "my dear grandfather," with all the details. Then perhaps he will answer.

[Not many people today.]

Mechin: I did rather regularly the exercise of "filling up." It fatigued me. I had headaches during the day. Must I continue?

Gurdjieff: Continue. You shall pass this crisis, your salvation is within. You must succeed in breaking down something. Do not be sparing; this fatigue can give you subtlety. You are strong like a pig. But for our work one must be a goat, a young goat is very good, an old goat, a bad odour. *[To the doctor]* I am sorry that you arrived late; I spoke concerning a medical question. I do the contrary of the usual doctor; he is not nervous; I make him nervous; the doctor nurses this; I aggravate it. He has everything except this thing. He is a bull, but not a purebred bull. It is necessary to change into a purebred bull. If you do not change, you will remain like an old goat. A moveable source of horrible emanations. Often you see, doctor, among your patients . . .

Pomereu: I have the impression of having more and more difficulty in the exercise of Sunday. I do not succeed in giving a shock to the chest and the vertebral column.

Gurdjieff: You know why it is difficult?

Pomereu: I don't know; probably because I work too much with my head.

Gurdjieff: You have not interest; you do not work with your being. You want to do it only theoretically . . . not *you*. You have decided by chance with your head, but it is not *you* who desires. It is necessary now for you to have one aim with all your being; if you work like this, then you shall wake this function up a little; you do not feel because you have not sentiment.

Among others, I say a thing that is not for you and at the same time is for you. I have ascertained this afternoon a thing which can render great service to all of you. It is an instinct which is not decayed. They are of good breeding. You are of a degenerate class. When you say "simple persons," it is that they are not yet degenerated. You do not have that normal thing that all the animals have. You notice it is simple people; for this I say, they are purebred, not degenerate; it is badly educated, it is simple. This thing that we have begun with you, it would be well to return to something ancient or it would be well for something new to be born in you. You can already begin to see on the seventh time that you come to me. You do not have contact or you do not poison yourself, one or the other, in order to go towards your aspirations. It is possible to have a common contact through the aim. It is possible with practice. For example, when you are seated together do not spend your time internally like in life. Use this occasion to do an exercise; suggest to yourself that this atmosphere about you, wakes up the desire to go towards the aim . . . everybody here. This atmosphere is warming for an aspiring with all your being towards a common aim. When you find yourselves together, suddenly, automatically it produces this heating. You can have a reciprocal action on a whole city. Paris is big; but if you begin it will become, little by little, possible that, if one movement is produced in a corner of this atmosphere, it will start an unrest which will spread over all.

You have knowledge of different telepathic acts. It is as if the atmosphere became large; a material is formed like in the web of a spider. If, in one of the meshes, a new force enters, this can correspond in the whole network, like in a electric conduit. It is necessary, when you are accidentally together, that you do an exercise. You create a factor of inclination for succeeding in your aim with all your mass. For this it is necessary that two things happen, auto-suggestion and representation by forms, but subjective forms. In the beginning you will understand what is happening; it is not important to picture it to oneself exactly. Imagine that in you there is a network. If one current comes in one point, it shall arrive everywhere, if one sensation of warmth is in one point, all the points shall feel the heat, the cold. Picture how what happens in one place happens everywhere.

Lanctin: In the weeks that just slipped away, I tried to make two parts well-carved in my life. I tried to arrange my external life as a function of the internal work that I had decided on, and to no longer do this work in the moments left free by life. The centre of this work is the exercise of "filling up" which allows me to reach a form in which I can always find myself. But I encounter, as soon as I have life, two obstacles. My body and my head. My body is an obstacle that I know. I know how to conquer it. But what I cannot conquer is my head, my attention. I do not see how to destroy this obstacle. In forcing, I succeed always in a result, but I feel that I force wrong.

Gurdjieff: You know that with your body you could sooner or later succeed. The head does not exist; it is the *result* of the body.

Lanctin: But when the body is completely passive . . .

Gurdjieff: With your head you can; with your head you cannot . . . but head is body.

Lanctin: With the body I see what to do; not with the head.

Gurdjieff: Work *with* the body; *for* your body.

Lanctin: You forget the head.

Gurdjieff: If the body changes, the head will change . . . with another body, another head. If you feel already something with your body, continue. The head shall follow the body.

Mme de Salzmann: The head must do nothing; it must be there as a witness. It shall train itself to remember.

Gurdjieff: It will serve you as an aid to recall. The role of your head is to be present. The service of your head is to be a constant witness. Bit by bit, it will no longer be away. With this you can change. It is very good advice.

Kahn: I have the feeling of this exercise. I feel things, I filled. But I lose the inspiration; I have nervous contractions which I cannot conquer.

Gurdjieff: You do not have the rhythm. It is necessary to do different things. (1) Inhale normally; (2) Retain the air while becoming discontracted; (3) Exhale without becoming contracted. It is not necessary to relax when you retain.

Kahn: I always have contracted exhalations.

Gurdjieff: You do not have rhythm, perhaps you have other disharmonies.

Kahn: You had told me to breathe some water; I have always one nostril that stops up.

Gurdjieff: You must continue. If you have been ill all your life, it is not possible to recover in one week. You have already change; before, it was always the same nostril that stopped up. Doctor, it is an original thing that this organic thing disappears. It goes to another place, thus there is no illness; and nevertheless illness. All doctors that hear, say there is sickness; I say that this thing can disappear and go elsewhere, here or here . . . If not illness, then what is it? It is an absurd original thing, but the patient understands it.

Kahn: Already before, I had the impression that if I was guided I would succeed in making this contraction disappear.

Gurdjieff: Continue that and do the new special exercise. To begin you take your watch and you divide your time exactly into three parts, not more than ten seconds each, between five and ten seconds; and not often, two or three times in twenty-four hours.

Kahn: Not in life?

Gurdjieff: With the exercise it is best. You put half the attention.

Paquer: How can I know and determine if I am identified with the work?

Gurdjieff: You must never work more than one-third of your state of awakeness; if during the other two-thirds you think about it, then you are identified. It is easy to recollect.

Aboulker: You told me that there are some times to detest my parents . . . now I can do it. Now I understand that I must detest the idea that I have of them and that I ought to live as if I had always been an orphan.

Gurdjieff: Do you pity yourself in these moments?

Aboulker: On the contrary, I receive some force from them.

Gurdjieff: What force?

Aboulker: The force of having to rely only on myself.

Gurdjieff: You have heard my explanation? You have felt that I was content or not content?

Aboulker: Since you spoke to me of it a long time ago, you must know what must happen.

Gurdjieff: Remember to ask Mme de Salzmann. What time is it? Try now to do this exercise of forming a web. The whole brotherhood also did the same thing. You know the proverb: "one for all, all for one." In ordinary life, this is a lie, because it is not realisable. But here is a brotherhood. They all have one common aim. One of them is there; but he must desire that all attain it, and inversely, the others are also obliged to help him. This example approaches that which one must do. This shall assist you in receiving a contact. Even egoistically one must desire it, because, in every feeble state, one shall be aided. One could say that, word for word, it is like in a cobweb.

Mme Thezenas: Can the weakest be aided thus?

Gurdjieff: This is not the subject. One is only excited. There exist two things; matter and force. This exercise is to urge, to excite, to animate.

[After dinner.]

Gurdjieff: Blonde number two, is there something new with your health? Good or bad, this does not exist. Only change exists.

Mme Vie: I have more headaches.

Gurdjieff: One sometimes calls bad that which is good. Before, you never had headaches; thus, it is very good. Perhaps what I have has produced an awakening. Your brain had not blood. The blood never passed through there; now the blood passes through, and so you have pain.

Mme Vie: I await . . .

Gurdjieff: It interests me to know this. You must not wait; sometimes the unhappiness of others makes me happy.

Mechin: I forgot to ask you something. In the exercise of "filling," I have difficulty in filling up the thighs.

Gurdjieff: What did you call it? Oh, the legs. We are going to speak about the legs. Change nothing in what I have explained. You have only to conquer the pig more and it must become a goat. Perhaps now the pig is in a very good path. Perhaps it only remains for the leg to change. Do not put special attention on that which concerns your leg. Sooner or later it shall be done. You have another quality now; do not separate the thighs from the head. All that shall be done.

Mme T: I succeed in doing the "filling" with a very very strong acuteness.

Gurdjieff: It is perhaps the first time that you have put all your conscience there. But first, what exercise are you doing?

Mme T: The "filling."

Gurdjieff: You were there when I explained it?

Mme T: No, Mme de Salzmann explained it to me.

Gurdjieff: Oh, Mme de Salzmann. The whole process happens without me. I am as if I fell from the moon.

Mme T: I feel the exercise very well, but I have the impression that it is a drudgery. In the beginning it interested me because it was new.

Gurdjieff: Do you have an aim for which you are doing, in general, all these things?

Mme T: Yes, I have an aim.

Gurdjieff: I have always regarded you as a visitor. It is now necessary to have a little knowledge. What is your aim?

Mme T: To succeed in being oneself.

Gurdjieff: You are not? You have a suspicion that you can succeed in being? So . . . It is still too soon for you to do an exercise. You can receive much from them but you do not have sufficient preparation to do them. You shall do only one exercise—two or three times in twenty-four hours: Relax consciously. You allow your thought, like a policeman, to verify everywhere that your muscles are not contracted. There exist three qualities of muscles: large, medium, small. You shall spend a week in relaxing each category of muscle. When you are sure that you can really relax completely, then you shall return to me and you shall re-*ask* your question. Not "lay down", *ask* . . . Can you explain to me in French; "lay down" and *ask?* To "lay down" is already for definite internal things. You can never "lay down" a question. A cigarette you can "lay down"; never "lay down" a question. We are speaking of what concerns bread . . . "lay down"; but a question is of different quality; *ask* a question, not "lay down." Definite things you can "lay down." If you are a French language professor, Mme, I am . . .

Mme de Salzmann: Are there any questions to be asked?

Dr. Blano: While I am working I have the impression of the complete disappearance of my physical body. I feel two distinct things; one which is more vast than my usual proportions and of which I know not the limits. The other, more internal, more limited, capable of directing me and which does not have a precise form, although it is comparable to my body.

Gurdjieff: That which you explain, now, does not resemble our work. If you continue, you have a fine chance of soon being a candidate for an insane asylum. It is a state which the spiritualists and theosophists know. Stop immediately. You must not forget that you are a body. You must always remember your body. You have not as yet an "I," no "me." Do not forget it. Thus only can you have a future. Later your body will have to have a real "I," a real "me" as every normal man should have. Now you feel the absence of body, no?

Blano: Yes

Gurdjieff: Well, you must feel your body ten times more. It is not necessary to leave your body. It is necessary to strengthen it. Many people exist like you; they are psychopaths.

Blano: How can I intensify the sensation of my body when I feel that it is leaving?

Gurdjieff: Wash your head in cold water. Do a difficult gymnastic. For example, hold your arms crosswise fifteen, twenty minutes, a half hour, while thinking "I am," "I want to be." Think it with the body. Feel your body. Drive out all the psychopathic associations; these are sickness, weakness.

Yahne: It seems to me that I am more and more physical. My only consciousness is that of my sensations. In my ordinary life and in my exercises, I experience the discomfort of being glued to my functions and of not being able to detach myself from them. How can I attain a more spiritual life?

Gurdjieff: Yahne, what you ask, what you want, I understand it. You do not have internal psychism of feeling. You want to strengthen this. I am going to give you two exercises which are for you only, no one else. It is necessary to separate your organic functions from your individuality. At the moment when you are working, when you self-remember, you have another state from the usual. It is necessary to separate these two states. For this there is an exercise, a whole series of exercises even. Here is the first: you do it, for example, seated, leaning comfortably installed in an arm-chair or on a couch. There is a spot where the arms are attached to the body (region of the shoulders), and a spot where the legs are attached to the body (hip joint); feel and control these four spots all the time. All your attention must be concentrated there. Send everything else to the devil. When you say "I am" imagine that these four spots are like four pillars on which is supported your "I am." Focus your attention; not on the extremities nor to the interior of the body. All your concentration is fixed on these four places. Do this for your future real "me." To begin, learn to know this state; it is like a measure, a clue. You will self-remember when you can feel well these four places. Leave all the rest. Live life as before. This is your only exercise, but do it very seriously so that all of the most concentrated moments of your work be based on those spots. After, you shall have title to a real individuality. These things could only serve as a barrier between your individuality and your ex-functions. I say "ex" because you must have a new quality of functions. The whole world must have a new quality of functions—because of an abnormal life in the past. It is necessary to create a barrier. For you, it shall be the result of this exercise. When you feel and are conscious of this definite barrier, your ground shall be prepared for a new exercise; then you will be able to have a new interior, independent, and a new exterior, independent. You shall have a normal body and a normal psychism, without the abnormal ex-functions. This is solely for her and for no one else. Do not try to do it out of curiosity. It is a very dangerous thing.

Hignette: I would like to ask how I could be sure that I am self-remembering and that I am working with my three centres. I have understood, theoretically, the necessity for this operation, but I would like to know if there exists a criterion for it.

[Later.]

It was less a question than a doubt; I do not know if it is worth asking.

Gurdjieff: You have understood that it was a naïve thing which you asked? Never read spiritualistic books. This leads to psychopathy, to insane asylums. Who has a question to ask?

Mme Dubeau: After each time that I work, I have a big revolt and at the same time I am very tired in my body. The physical carries along the psychical, and I do not succeed in emerging from it.

Gurdjieff: It is the scarcity of cold water. You do not like to do this. It is important reason for bringing up a conflict. The organism does not like it. The head alone, perhaps, asks it. It is the real reason for your revolt. It does not know it perhaps, but this is so. The head looks for explanations, for reasons . . . The body is very spoiled, very indolent. Each day now you have a different psychic state. Continue for a week, and now with the coldest water.

Mme Dubeau: I gave up everything two days ago.

Gurdjieff: Forget now that you have not done it for two days. Your body must ask excuses from your spirit. If it pardons, I shall pardon also. Act as if you had been sick during these two days. Now I advise a new thing: each day buy, for five francs, some ice and put it in water.

Mme Dubeau: But, Mr. Gurdjieff, it seems to me that all this that I am doing, the whole instruction depends on the will of the head. This grows weaker, and in a moment all snaps.

Gurdjieff: Your head cannot will for a long time. When the accumulator is discharged, stop. Only, you decide; I do not want this animal to dominate me. Pardon, it is your indolent animal: it is like a cat, a dog, a mouse. Now you know that you cannot be in yourself a long time. All that is dignified in man is submissive to this animal.

Mme Dubeau: Yet, I find good reasons for being in revolt against the work. I lose all my illusions and I have nothing tangible in exchange.

Gurdjieff: The whole world submits to it. You are part of your stool, and you are not still seated on another. We regret it. It is a very bad state to be between two stools. Believe me. Buy a mirror; after that, another life shall begin and another illusion.

Mme Dubeau: In life, when people do you harm, must one say to oneself, "I don't care; it is not harmful," or defend oneself against them?

Gurdjieff: A bit of good advice: look at each of these occasions as a way of working in order to enlarge your will. It is very easy. You know what relations you used to have earlier, automatically. Today reply consciously, make yourself known consciously.

Mme Dubeau: But in the same way?

Gurdjieff: As you wish. Bad, good, this does not exist. The result of this shall be to charge your accumulator for the next demonstration. The more consciously you do this, the more energy you shall have; and that which appeared impossible to you will appear better than expected.

Boussique: Indeed, these last times, I have tried that. I ascertained that at that time I had no more identifications or negative emotions, that I had closed off impressions of the other kind and that I was accusing myself.

Gurdjieff: First you must feel clearer and stop your "idiocy." Then you will increase the energy in your accumulator.

Mme Dupré: Can everybody do this exercise?

Gurdjieff: That is a good object. I am happy that you perceive it. Control each act. If you remember to do it consciously and not automatically, you shall have a result quite different.

Aboulker: I would like to ask you a question on remorse. It is very difficult for me to feel remorse. Example: one imagines that he loves his parents. The work shows you your egoism and this assists you in stirring up remorse; but for me, I have not had any illusions about myself for a long time, since the age of fourteen or fifteen perhaps. The work has showed me that there were in some things that I believed entirely egoistical, something other than egoism.

Gurdjieff: You cannot have the future that you want without retrieving the past. If you remain as you are, you can have no future. For example, you say that the work has showed you a part in you that is not absolutely egoistical.

Aboulker: I don't feel, today, a grain of love for my neighbour.

Gurdjieff: Ah, that is another question. Take something other than egoism.

Aboulker: Having never had illusions about the value of my sentiments as a son, as a brother, these ascertainings do not give me impulse to stir up remorse.

Gurdjieff: You have looked here only at big things. It is necessary to look now at the small. Your worthlessness is related to small

143

things. Certain, positive little things, by degrees. One must make a beginning; egoism is a big thing.

Aboulker: I do not want to venture out in a hackneyed way. This is why I ask assistance.

Gurdjieff: I understood, doctor, I sincerely understood your need. When you change, when you become different, you cannot see it. When you say I could not see it; who cannot, which one? You are many; in you, there is not one but many people. Try to make some statistics. You are four people. Which can see, which cannot? When?

Aboulker: In the biggest majority of cases, it is the habitual me that sees the habitual me.

Gurdjieff: The "habitual me" is not always the same; for example, when you have eaten well . . . Usually we speak of the three functions. Today I tell you that you are four. There are even seven of them in all. In you, there is a function: that of sex. Take these four functions; thoughts, emotions, instinct, sex. When the one is boss, when it directs and governs all, how does it see, or does it not see?

Aboulker: I do not understand well . . .

Gurdjieff: Reflect for two days. It is not necessary to reply immediately. Until the present I had spoken of your three functions, today I speak of the fourth which influences you even more than your food. Food has less influence for the individual than this fourth, than sex. Today, your power is below its subordination. You are a function of this thing.

Aboulker: How does one overcome this thing? Isn't that "to see oneself"?

Gurdjieff: I have given you this principle. Perhaps you have chosen, in order to look at your past life, a line in which this quality of yourself or ego was absent. Now I advise you to usher it in, to take it into account; also in your observations of your past. Even in your relations with your father.

Aboulker: Madame, I do not completely understand what is this fourth factor?

Mme de Salzmann: Sex.

Aboulker: My attitude with my patients; absence of love, professional sentiment. One time last year I felt something else. I would like to discover it.

Gurdjieff: I have given you a key to search your past. You have a sexual state always different. What result do you have in one state? What results in another? Observe from this point of view. These results will give you a different value. Now do you understand?

Aboulker: Yes, Monsieur.

Gurdjieff: He who had initiative in the past was this Monsieur. The observations will unfold for you a secret and this secret will open up a hole from which will depart the remorse of conscience.

Aboulker: I apologise but I am always afraid of not being understood.

Gurdjieff: Sometimes I have the appearance of not having understood. It is because I want to bring you to understand something else.

Aboulker: I fear that I am being laughed at.

Gurdjieff: I haven't dealt a single blow to your body with my feet. Doctor, I want to make you see in your life two sides; one side, filthy, and one side, filthier. What interests me is that you see yourself. I would not even desire to give you the impulsion for that. That must come from you, from you alone. Until the next time, you shall think about this new idea which I give you. You shall put your question to me again, later; perhaps I shall reply to you aside.

Mlle de Gaigneron: I would like to know from where comes this internal voice which dictates to us our acts and which is more sure and steady than instinct.

Gurdjieff: Philip, how are you? You have grown again a little bit. Three months of absence; now you are already all changed. When one does not see children for a certain time, one notices that they grow. I know many children that have become young women, men. There are even some who have aged.

[At the beginning, the net exercise while waiting for Mr. Gurdjieff. He arrives later, speaks with Mme de Salzmann and then—]

Gurdjieff: It would interest me very much to know something about your self-remembering. How does this work go? Do you often forget? Is it easy, difficult, or something else? Are you pulled into life, and do you do it often? Or not often? Who does it? How? What value do you give to self-remembering? I would like someone to tell me how he behaves in regard to this.

G.B: I have the impression that my self-remembering is not voluntary. It is given to me at certain moments. I would like to do it in the moments when it is difficult, and when I am unable to do it.

Gurdjieff: It is not a question of that. You have the task of remembering yourself. We do it as a task. Do you understand?

G.B: Not very well.

Gurdjieff: Do you forget?

G.B: Sometimes I am in a good state and I do it well . . .

Gurdjieff: The state is one thing and self-remembering another thing. It is the business of the head. Do you remember yourself often, or forget yourself often?

G.B: Both. I do it often during the day. At times I decide to do it suitably resting; and I forget. And also very often, I do it without having decided in advance.

Gurdjieff: In other words you forget to remember yourself when it is necessary; but when it is useless you remember yourself automatically. This is not our aim at all. One must accustom oneself to self-remembering consciously. You will not succeed unless you make the task of remembering yourself with your whole presence— at for example, four o'clock, five o'clock and six o'clock, and say "I am."

Mme D: I do not understand how it is possible to remember oneself in life. Already in self-remembering under the best conditions, in stopping myself, in quieting myself—I reach with so much difficulty such a little thing—that I can say I never remember myself in life.

Gurdjieff: Then you do nothing consciously. You do automatically all that you do.

Mme D: Then what to do, Monsieur?

Gurdjieff: Give yourself as task: "All or nothing." If you cannot do that you are nothing. You must achieve that.

Mme D: I have done it.

Gurdjieff: One must take as a task to remember oneself.

Mme D: But how to remember oneself since even in the best conditions I do not achieve it?

Gurdjieff: The worse the conditions the better the result. It is for this that one must do. Do not consider the conditions; consider the moment of decision. At each of the three hours, you absolutely must remember yourself. You enter into yourself; you feel that you exist with all your presence and this—this is your task. Afterwards you break it all. One cannot always self-remember. What counts is to do it consciously. With an automatic decision that is worth nothing.

Mme D: I do not understand, Monsieur, how you wish me to understand the word "consciously," since never . . .

Mme de Salzmann: Because you have decided intentionally in advance—you feel that it is conscious.

Mme D: But the word has no meaning for me.

Mme de Salzmann: Intentionally in advance.

Mme D: The sensation is not strong. I have done it like that.

Gurdjieff: Your decision is not strong. You must decide many things. You must put yourself in a quiet state—relaxed—and in this state settle your task. You try it. Ten times, a hundred times, you fail. You continue. You take trouble. Little by little you train yourself and you achieve it. But not in one effort. This is a very little thing; and it is the most important. Remember yourself consciously. *Consciously.* That is to say, by your own decision. To remember oneself and at the same time, collect oneself together, to penetrate deeply into one's very self—these then are the conditions. If you cannot continue for a long time, try it for a short time.

Mme D: I never enter deeply into myself.

Gurdjieff: At the start never?

Mme D: I do not succeed.

Gurdjieff: You do not do it. Already you have not understood "consciously"—you have said so yourself. Then do it.

Mme B: Why? I do not succeed, Mr. Gurdjieff.

Mme de Salzmann: At the beginning you must do it by your own decision, not by chance, not because it happened to come to your mind. But you have taken the decision to do it at a certain moment, and you do it.

Mme D: But I do it like this.

Gurdjieff: You do it badly. Do this in the same way that you have given yourself your promise to be here at seven o'clock. This is an example. If you do not do it like this it has no value at all. Give yourself your promise and do. You give yourself your promise in this way to remember yourself at a certain moment.

Mme D: I do it like this, but I act automatically. My decision is automatic. I do not succeed in feeling like a human being.

Gurdjieff: You must do an exercise to be more collected. Learn to collect yourself. Choose a good moment that seems propitious. Sit down. Let nobody disturb you. Relax yourself. All your attention—all your will is concentrated on your relaxation. You quieten your associations. After—only after, you begin to think.

Mme D: Yes. I try like that and I do not succeed.

Gurdjieff: Wait. Do not disturb me—do not interrupt me. You have never done like this. Your explanations prove it to me. After, when you have quietened your associations, only then, begin the exercise—consciously, with all your attention, all your faculties.

You represent to yourself that you are surrounded by an atmosphere. Like the earth, man also has an atmosphere, which surrounds him on all sides, for a metre, more or less—to a limit. In the atmosphere the associations, in ordinary life the thoughts—produce waves. It concentrates at certain places—it recedes; it has movements according to the direction which you impart to it. This depends on the movement of your thought. Your atmosphere is displaced in the direction in which your thought goes. If you think of your mother, who is far away your atmosphere moves towards the place where your mother is. When you do this exercise, you represent to yourself that this atmosphere has limits. For example one metre and a half, shall we say. Then you concentrate all your attention on preventing your atmosphere from escaping beyond the limit. You do not allow it to go further than one metre or one metre and a half. When you feel your atmosphere quietened, without waves, without movement, then with all your will you suck it into yourself—you conserve yourself in this atmosphere. You draw it consciously into yourself. The more you can, the better it is. To start with, it is very tiring.

That is how one must do the exercise. Afterwards you rest yourself—you send the exercise to the devil. Repeat it afresh in the evening. This exercise is done especially to allow one to have a collected state. It is the first exercise. It is difficult to penetrate into yourself at the first effort. One must compel the atmosphere to remain within its limits—not allow it to go further than it should. It is the first exercise in order to have a collected state. This exercise I have given to everybody. No one has understood what is collectedness, nor given it attention.

I have seen this from the way you speak. When you have succeeded in doing that, you will be able to have a truly good state, and you will be able, by your will—to re-enter completely into yourselves.

When you say "I am" you will sense that you are in yourself, you will sense in the whole of the body—the echo of "I"—and when you say "am" you will have the sensation, completely, that you are you. But if you do for ten years "I am—I am—I am" it will lead you to nothing but to be a candidate for the madhouse. Do that or nothing. Begin everything again with that exercise. It is the first exercise for remembering oneself.

Mme D: Will I really feel this atmosphere without any doubt—without asking myself if this is not imagination—because I do all the exercises like this. I go, I go and I stop myself; I ask myself if I have not wholly imagined. I do not wish any more to imagine.

Gurdjieff: You have not yet done this exercise. Do it. Only he who does can judge the results in himself.

Mme D: I have done it, Mr. Gurdjieff has given it to G.B.

Gurdjieff [to G.B.]: Have I given it to you? What results have you obtained?

G.B: The remembering was better. I have felt better the "I."

Gurdjieff: You have felt it?

G.B: Yes, but the intensity of remembering in me decreases very quickly.

Gurdjieff: Have you really done this for a long time regularly?

G.B: I have not done it over a long time.

Gurdjieff: You have done it only for several days?

G.B: No longer.

Gurdjieff: I do not understand how it can diminish. When you are in the state of remembering—half of your attention must be concentrated on the "I am" and the other half must control the keeping of the state. Your head plays the role of policeman. It watches for you, to guard your state. "I am" with the other half of the attention. The other part supervises.

G.B: But the power of control mounts and then declines.

Gurdjieff: You have not done it as I have told you. Half of your attention must supervise—but you leave the associations to go on. Your thought parades in the room in Paris. It goes into another country. Your atmosphere—your imagination leaves you, and you remain with your automatic attention. Done in this way it is normal that it diminishes. One must do thousands and thousands of times what I tell you.

G.B: On the other hand, I have noticed that my remembering is better if it is less frequent.

Gurdjieff: This is a small thing. First of all get used to staying a long time in a collected state. It is this that is absent in you. What you say is a small thing. When you have done what I tell you, you will be able to do a thousand times more.

P: Mr. Gurdjieff, I have noticed that if I achieve very intense remembering when I do the exercises, the opposite happens in ordinary life: if I try to play a role or to remember myself when I am with other people, the result is much more superficial.

Gurdjieff: I have explained it a thousand times. You must never use in life the results of work, so long as these results are not fixed in you. Use nothing, hope for nothing.

[Mr. Gurdjieff speaks in Russian with Mme de Salzmann.]

P: Must one limit oneself to the exercise or must one also play a role?

Gurdjieff: Also. A man who works is always seeking for means to do. If you meet a great many people you can make use of it. This will make something grow in you if you do it well.

P: What does it mean to play a role? Does it mean to behave in front of other people as though one did not work?

Mme de Salzmann: Mr. Gurdjieff has said it a hundred times:

internally not to identify, externally to do everything as before, as though nothing has changed; but consciously, instead of letting oneself be carried along.

Gurdjieff: And do it so that nobody notices any change in you and that you are doing some special internal work. The important work for you is to try not to be identified. Externally, you continue to do all that life demands. But you play a role. What occupies the whole of you is your internal work. To be able to work, one must not be identified internally. Externally do all you are obliged to do in public. But do not come out from within yourself; play a role. Consciously, do all you have to do.

Question: I experience in self-remembering something which, I believe is not new. I experience a more intense sensation in the sense of stronger affirmation.

Gurdjieff: What do you mean?

Question: I mean that my self-remembering has changed in this sense. Then, suddenly, I seem to be deprived of all energy, empty. And I sleep like a mass.

Gurdjieff: No, wait, I want to translate your word.

Question: Affirmation?

Gurdjieff: What? What does it do?

Question: The voluntary impulse is much stronger.

[Mme de Salzmann speaks in Russian to Mr. Gurdjieff.]

Gurdjieff: You do it too long.

Question: No.

Gurdjieff: One must not work for long. Stop and do something else. Stop yourself before falling asleep, I have already said that—stop as soon as you begin to feel tired.

Question: I am not sleepy when I begin the exercise. Then, suddenly, my energy fails.

Gurdjieff: An association sucks away your energy.

Question: Everything stops.

Gurdjieff: Don't do too much. Do better as to quality, and less as to quantity.

Question: But I already work very little.

Gurdjieff: Do everything little by little. When you work consciously, and even half-consciously, it eats your energy. You have only one accumulator, not ten. It is recharged when you sleep, and then you eat up the energy. It all goes. One should not leave the lamps burning too long.

Question: One should spend less energy in external life to have more left for the work.

Gurdjieff: It has nothing to do with it. Don't concern yourself with that. External work goes on quite automatically and requires very little energy. Let life go on by itself. Keep your energy for work. Work needs a lot of energy.

Mlle D: Mr. Gurdjieff, I told you last week that I was a slave to my pity. You gave me as exercise to remember myself, arms in the form of a cross, for five minutes, adding a minute every day. Through this exercise I managed to become calmer. I had a sensation of pain and at the same time an organic sensation of self-remembering, yet not very deep. I don't co-ordinate. I feel now one now the other. Should I continue?

Gurdjieff: Yes, continue. After only a week I can say nothing. Sometimes a year or two years are necessary before one can say something.

P: Mr. Gurdjieff, my self-remembering, as a task in external life, has not changed. But in self-remembering when alone I observe the same thing as Mme F.—I go to sleep. My body escapes—I can't hold it.

Gurdjieff: You must struggle with yourself. In addition to your time spent on the exercise, do ten minutes with your arms in the form of a cross.

P: I have done that. But when I try to do the exercises once more, I feel sleepy again.

Gurdjieff: Rub yourself well with cold water afterwards. If that does not help, tell me; I shall give you some "bird's tongue".

[Mr. Gurdjieff explains that "bird's tongue" is dwarf red peppercorns.]

When one has tasted them, one never forgets them. It wakes you up at night. I shall give you two or three peppercorns to keep by. But before you try it, try rubbing yourself with cold water.

[Conversation in Russian between Mr. Gurdjieff and Mme de Salzmann.]

Mme de Salzmann: If you divide your attention rightly, one part to relax, another part to concentrate, you couldn't go to sleep. Sleep comes if all your attention goes only on relaxing.

Gurdjieff: In her case it is work that makes her sleepy. In his [D.] case it is because he divides badly. On one side, he gives his associations freedom to wake up. These are quite different things. He said "for me as for her," but the reason is not the same. She really works and loses energy, but in your case the reason is that you work badly, incorrectly.

H: Mr. Gurdjieff, sometimes I get bored with self-remembering. I wait with impatience for the end of the time I have set for the exercise. It is monstrous. Yet I can't help it. Sometimes I feel a wonderful fullness, but at other times absolutely nothing. I can't help it and when this state comes I don't know to what it is due.

Gurdjieff: This proves that automatism is very strong in you, that you have many weaknesses, many dogs, many "results to de-salt." You must kill them. How can one be bored with a divine thing?

H: Something is lacking in my self-remembering.

Gurdjieff: It is a symptom of the fact that you have nasty things in you. All this has to be cleaned up to become worthy of doing this exercise. Put ten times more attention on cleaning up your inside and making it worthy. You are not worthy. There are too many dogs. Do you understand what I call dogs? Different things crystallised in you by life, by education. All these results play the role of factors creating associations which arise continually and carry us with them. These factors are many. It is impossible to kill them outright. But we must turn them into functions. At present one of these factors often becomes your "I" and guides you. Until real "I" comes, its place must be held by the head—the head must play the role of "I."

Mlle D: Mr. Gurdjieff, when I remember myself, I never experience a feeling of complete satisfaction. The more I concentrate, the nearer I feel to it, but something separates me and, in the end, I have rather a feeling of uneasiness and disgust.

Gurdjieff: Disgust of what?

Mlle D: Disgust of myself, disgust . . .

[A silence.]

Gurdjieff: Can you stay a moment after the meeting? I shall tell you what makes you uneasy.

H: Mr. Gurdjieff, how to recognise these dogs, how to know which are the worst? And then, must one attack them, and how? Or should I continue with the general procedure?

Gurdjieff: Generally, in everyone these dogs are accustomed to live around the centres. It is their place. Factors become crystallised according to the predominant centre. We have four centres, four localities, four villages where these dogs live. In one village they are many, in another village fewer, in yet another they are very few. In different people there are a greater or lesser number of dogs in each village. These villages are: thought, feeling, sensation and sex—which is a very important village. One person has more dogs in one village, another in another. It depends on which village has more inhabitants. My advice, since you have asked me . . . Repeat your question.

[H. repeats his question.]

In general, in order to kill the dogs so that they do not trouble you any more, and have no longer the power to get hold of your "I," my advice is the following (it goes for everybody): The first thing is to get rid of the dogs in the village of sex. Then in the others. But first you must liquidate this intimate animal. Later you will transfer your attention to other villages. If you know this rule, you will look to find with which village to continue. But how to tie them? First of all you set yourself the task of never letting the dogs go on as before. Hit them at once on the head. Once you have recognised your enemy your task is to fight it. Perhaps it is your real enemy. One after another you master all these dogs. And then you pass on to another village. In this way you will gradually overcome all your enemies. I repeat, it is not a question of killing them. If something is crystallised, it is for ever. It may even prove an asset if you use it as material, as function. But they must never take the upper hand, they must never be allowed to fix your "I" and get possession of it. This should be your task. And this applies to all of you here.

H: Mr. Gurdjieff, this sex function is a function? It is not something one must reduce and flatten as much as possible?

Gurdjieff: We are not speaking of functions which are parts of us, but of dogs, that is, of weaknesses around our functions. Functions are the villages—one cannot change them. As to dogs, yes, one must change their breed.

P: I suppose there are more dogs in a weaker village. Is it so?

Gurdjieff: Perhaps the village becomes weak because it has many dogs to weaken it. Each dog has a name in these villages. I know all their names.

[Mr. Gurdjieff jokes about the dogs' names.]

Once I gave an exercise, but I see that nobody has done it and that it led to no results. I shall repeat it. Maybe there is someone more intelligent who will understand it and crystallise. It is the exercise of filling the body. Maybe someone remembers? *I am.* When you say "I," you get an echo. Everyone understands what this sensation is. In this exercise it is not a question of that. One has to sense this echo first in the right leg, then in the left leg, then in the right arm, then in the left, the abdomen, the thorax. Do this series three times. Then the head—once. Three times the whole, and once the head. And repeat if you have time. Twice in the six places. The third time in seven places.

P: Must one listen long for the breathing? One tends to do it with breathing . . .

Gurdjieff: Don't do it with breathing. It would give you a wrong tempo. Take the necessary time for breathing and for sensing. It will then be your measure. You understand? Represent to yourselves, then sense in your right leg, then change. Don't pay attention to breathing. The tempo will establish itself. It depends on many things, on tiredness, on many other things. Breathing has nothing to do with it. Don't connect it with this exercise.

D: Should one consider each limb in its totality in one respiration or several respirations for each?

Gurdjieff: Yes, each limb in its totality.

V: In saying "I" or "am"?

Gurdjieff: Both. But "I" is independent. You must sense its echo in the leg. You say "*I am,*" but, instead of sending the echo of "I" in the whole body, you sense it in the leg. Do this exercise entirely independently of the exercise of filling. Once you have done it, you will do the filling still better.

A: One must stop the sensation at the leg?

Gurdjieff: Yes, only the leg.

P: Should one say it aloud?

Gurdjieff: No, inside. Sense it. In this exercise the leg is the body. The rest plays the part of the head. Then the left leg plays the part of the body, and the rest, including the right leg, is the head.

P: Does one forget the body?

Gurdjieff: No, you sense it as your head. In place of the head—everything together.

Mme D: Wouldn't it be better, instead of doing all the exercises, to do only this one, for example, for a week?

Gurdjieff: If it is more convenient for you. I don't know your family circumstances. But these two exercises are good for you. These two exercises will allow you really to begin.

P: I have observed two things. The ideas produce very strong feelings in me. But I see very often that living beings have no ideas. And then I notice that I have no feelings for them.

Gurdjieff: What is your question?

P: My question, in a word, is—how to experience feeling, how to be human?

Gurdjieff: First of all you must feel that there are ideas and ideas. For instance, a madman may have the idea that he is Napoleon, or some similar big thing. He has an idea. What then are your ideas? If you have ideas, they are ideas of a madman. A man who has normal mentation will see that your idea is not a real idea. He has real ideas. You must understand this truth.

P: I don't understand very well.

Mme de Salzmann: Mr. Gurdjieff means that you believe in your ideas. You believe that they *are* ideas. You don't think that others, more normal, have real ideas.

P: But the presence of an idea in another man always moves me.

Mme de Salzmann: And Mr. Gurdjieff answers you that you are moved only if this idea is yours.

Gurdjieff: A madman who thinks he is Napoleon likes other madmen who believe they are Napoleons. They understand each other, they confer together! No. Think impartially about your idea. What is the quality of your idea? Why with a certain person it establishes a desirable contact between you, while with other people it establishes a contact that is not desirable? Analyse this impartially; when you have material concerning this question we shall speak about it and I shall say many useful things to you. I have some material regarding your question. In the course of my life I worked for fifteen years in a lunatic asylum where there were four thousand madmen, the largest asylum in the world near Tashkent.

P: I have made this observation to ask you this question: how to develop feeling?

Gurdjieff: Do what I tell you. This will awaken all the factors of your feeling, provided you are sincere, sincere with yourself. And provided you analyse impartially.

P: I don't quite understand. Impartial analysis of what?

Mme de Salzmann: Try to understand, through impartial analysis, what causes you to establish contact with some and not with others. Analyse it sincerely in yourself.

It is time. Mr. Gurdjieff gives you leave to go.

MEETING THIRTY
THURSDAY, 10 AUGUST 1944

[Mr. Gurdjieff had not arrived in the room and Mme de Salzmann asked for questions on the exercise given by Mr. Gurdjieff on the food eaten consciously.]

Question: This exercise has shown me in an extraordinary way, one side of myself. I had never met my mechanism in myself, as I have done in this exercise. My automatism, my animal. The first few times, I got the most from it. Later, I encountered difficulties. In the beginning this exercise showed me things in myself, which I have not been able to find later, as if the obstacles accumulated afterwards.

Mme de Salzmann: You no longer wish to do it?

Question: At first it gave me an intellectual shock. It was perhaps only intellectual. But I have not really succeeded with the exercise.

Mme de Salzmann: Do you continue?

Question: Not seriously. I have not succeeded in taking my meals alone. And it is impossible to think of doing it in company.

Question: In doing the exercise, I felt the point of application; which constitutes the food, the consolation, the satisfaction it gives to the lower nature. One consoles oneself for many things when eating. I have noticed too, the avidity with which one eats. And this exercise has also made me participate in all nature. I said to myself: what I eat is part of nature; who created this nature? Who created what I eat? I felt united with everything. This gave me interior impressions. A rest too, a fortification, a feeling of union. It did one good to feel that one can take impressions while eating, as real as those one takes with one's mind.

Mme de Salzmann: It gave you something?

Question: A great deal.

Mme de Salzmann: And always in a positive way? Nothing in you refused?

Question: There is such a difference between one's habits and this, it is so considerable. I do not say that I could never be otherwise, but anyway I shall always force myself to be like this.

Mme de Salzmann [to another]: And you?

Question: It has been rather difficult. It gives me a feeling of calm.

If I could concentrate afterwards, it would add to my presence. I feel the food passing like the air. It gives me a sensation of myself such as I have never had.

Mme de Salzmann [to another]: And you also?

Question: I cannot say that. Ah, I had forgotten; it destroys greed. One learns to take from the foods something other than pleasure.

Mme de Salzmann: At the same time it reinforces this.

Question: I have noticed that it gives more value to what one eats. I have understood that I eat too fast. It has given me more calm. One appreciates more. One is more aware of the quality. But it is more difficult to get the sensation in the œsophagus. I can in the mouth. Not in the œsophagus.

[Mr. Gurdjieff comes in and Mme de Salzmann translates.]

Gurdjieff: If I can speak by analogy, I should say that you come to the crux of the idea, that before you were no different from Mr. Dog or Mr. Cat. And now, you constate that you are a little different.

Question: A very big difference.

Gurdjieff: A difference; you are a human being, not a dog. Man knows how to eat. How? Consciously. He knows how to direct, assimilate not like a dog. Only after this, man can cease to be called a factory for merde; until then, everyone is a factory for merde. As for you, doctor, what you say that you now feel that it is an impression, this is exactly what I mean when I say we have a third food. That is it. You have a taste of what third food is. There is the food which enters by the mouth. That which enters by the nose, and that which enters by the *[Mr. Gurdjieff indicates his head].* These are the impressions, the third food. Without these, man is a dog, an automaton. He really is a dog. Every day, he needs the food of impressions. So you can now say without anxiety, that you are not a dog, but that you are in the image of God. *[To another]* Do you continue?

Question: At first it went very well, and now it goes very badly. The first time, like the doctor, I was satisfied . . .

Gurdjieff: Do you continue?

Question: Afterwards, I did not take my meals alone. It is very difficult to do it in public, my head revolted.

Gurdjieff: Always, when one thing goes well, there appear at once in man some factors of opposition. One must struggle. The good force is the angel. The revolt is the devil. It is an automatic process of struggle. You must enter into this automatic process and help the angel or the devil. You have the taste of what is the good angel; favour the angel. Otherwise you will sell yourself to the devil.

Question: What has worried me this week is that I made categorical decisions concerning three things. The food exercise, the other exercises, and—

Gurdjieff: This is cheap, all these decisions. Always man decides, but his word is worth tuppence. Do what I say progressively; I know that you do not exist. It has to be done little by little. I know your weaknesses. One day your word will be true. Today you cannot keep your word. These categorical decisions? You can decide nothing categorically. If at the beginning you had done the exercise well, you should have continued; today you could have done something else. But your decision, anyone can make the same.

Question: What I do not understand, is that I have not been the same—

Gurdjieff: You must continue. If you stop the process, you destroy all the results you have acquired. Re-do everything. It is possible that it will become ten times more difficult. It is your fault. You stopped yourself. You must come to the state which you had at the beginning of the exercise. Without this state you can do nothing. Let us put this question aside. Who has some interesting questions? I think today is the day for questions.

Mme de Salzmann: You gave another exercise, the one of feeling the "I" in the seven parts of the body.

Gurdjieff: Did you do this exercise? You must have been surprised in the beginning. How can one feel one's "I" in the leg? Who can say that this is possible? Only he who has done it can say. Without practice it is absurd. Who has done it?

Question: I . . .

Gurdjieff: Say now.

Question: In the beginning it was very difficult to feel the "I," it was very long and then, once I had felt it in the right leg, it was easier in the other parts.

Gurdjieff: Did it now show you anything new, or suggest a question to you?

Question: Yes, it was that my legs took little part in the exercise, that the sensation at the solar plexus was stronger than in the rest of the body.

Gurdjieff: Well then, you do not need help, supplementary details? Then continue.

Question: I have really tried, but I have not succeeded. I did not succeed in relaxing myself. As soon as I tried to feel my "I" in the back of my head, I no longer felt relaxed. I no longer had the sensation of relaxation.

Gurdjieff: The reason: it is that you cannot relax yourself well. Before each exercise, you must take ten minutes to relax yourself.

Question: I tried. With the face I succeeded.

Gurdjieff: The face is a small thing. You must relax your whole presence, not only one part, to quieten associations.

Question: I thought that you had to relax one part after another, beginning with the top.

Gurdjieff: It is just the opposite. You must begin with the feet and go upwards. Try like that. You begin with the head, and it contracts again and the contraction descends everywhere. Begin again and relax from your feet.

Question: This exercise has defined for me a sensation which I had begun to experience with other exercises; the sensation of having an interior armature in my whole body. And at the same time . . .

Gurdjieff: Excuse me, explain better; "armature"? In electricity the whole of the wires and lamps is called armature. Is it this?

Question: No, I mean a force in the interior of my body which makes me feel the whole form of my body.

[Discussion follows on the word "armature."]

Gurdjieff: A skeleton?

Question: No, finer than the bones, with a circulation inside this thing.

Gurdjieff: Who understands here? Use another word.

Question [from another]: An internal solidity of the body. Before I did not feel it. Now I feel a thickness, more weight.

Gurdjieff [to the former questioner]: Is it this? Do you feel your body is thicker?

Question: It is difficult to explain all that I experienced. I cannot say thick, the twice that I did it I had a sensation of heat, light but clear. And that enabled me to do the exercise with lighter breathing.

Gurdjieff: But you speak of subjective things. That would last three evenings if each one did as much.

Question: It is a new sensation. I wish to know if it was right.

Gurdjieff: There is as yet no result. I cannot say anything. I have not understood. I cannot help you. Ask me some details. But the story of your subjective constatations does not interest anyone here.

Question: I have a question I wish to ask.

Gurdjieff: Well, begin without advertisement and do not waste time.

Question: I wanted to ask you if one should do like this. Before feeling my "I" in the seven parts of the body, I am obliged to feel it in my whole presence. Otherwise, the echo of the "I" remains intellectual. I have tried to do it directly, and the echo remained intellectual. I have tried to feel the "I" in all my presence. The echo came better. Should one do it like this?

Gurdjieff: No, lie down, well relaxed in all your parts, and you begin.

Question: At once?

Gurdjieff: After you are entirely relaxed, you do the exercise, feel your "I" in each part. And everywhere, there should be the same intensity, the same quantity, the same rhythm of breathing. So that there is no difference anywhere. Once you can do it separately in each part, then you can mobilise the whole: *"I am."*

You can repeat this many times. Do not philosophise. It is quite simple. One can only understand it and do it well, when one is completely relaxed. Many people have bad characters and are nervous. This relaxation will quieten them and will take away all they have in them which is futile and idiotic.

Question: You also gave us the exercise of retaining our emanations around us. Well, I cannot do this. I see how many things escape from me. My thought goes incessantly from the sphere which I try to form. Even when I am calm, stretched out, alone, even then things escape from the sphere.

Gurdjieff: It is a difficult exercise. One must relax and quieten oneself. If many associations present themselves, one must continue to relax, and send away without pausing all the associations connected with business, with exterior things. And even when you are quiet, you cannot do it completely all at once. It is only then that the exercise begins.

Question: This exercise has shown me that I have never known how to relax. This word has had no meaning for me until now. The relaxation depends on the whole "I," it is not only physical.

Gurdjieff: Yes, it is not only physical, it is the whole presence which is made up of different parts. When I say the whole presence, I mean the whole organism, the nervous system, the physical mechanism. All that, one must quiet it *consciously.* It is only possible consciously. Subconsciously one starts with associations in Asia or in America. One travels, one is here or there. Try not to start with your thought, in imagination. Try; stay here. Everything which interrupts you send to the devil. Even God, the angel, the devil, all that to the devil. Look upon the work of quietening yourself as the most important thing. It is only with this attitude that you will obtain a result. You will arrive at something. You will only get there by repetition, by beginning again a great number of times.

Question: There is another obstacle which I encounter in all the exercises; I mechanise them all. For instance, in the exercise of "I" in seven parts, I make a reckoning. I say to myself: I breathe three times for the foot, seven times for the leg. This makes the exercise easier, but it causes me to lose all the benefit. And in life I do the same thing. For everything which I do I make a reckoning in advance.

Gurdjieff: This is the fault of your professors of mathematics who taught you everything by repetition and nothing by comprehension. You must change this. In order to do this, it is necessary to do another exercise. Instead of the reckoning, do something else which is more difficult for your head. It is a pity you do not come on Mondays to the Salle Pleyel. What we do there would break your habit. Automatism must do four counts at once. You, you have the habit of doing one. There we do four. If you have to do four, it works out in this way, that one nail chases another.

Question: This exercise of keeping my atmosphere for myself has given me a very strong sensation of my presence. But I feel this presence for a very long time in the day, when the exercise is finished. This helps me very much in what I have to do. But you said one should not mix the work with life. Should I stop this?

Gurdjieff: Do not use this force. Let life flow as before. Do not mix the two states. In life, do not work beyond the time especially consecrated to the exercises.

Question: How do I stop this sensation of my presence?

Gurdjieff: Remind yourself of remorse of conscience. Make a vow before your ideal that you will not use this force in life. "If I do it, cause a pimple to grow on my nose." At the same time, you practise keeping your word. Punish yourself. One day, two days, ten days without food. Be thirsty. Make your body suffer. It must *do*. But when it has done what you have ordered it to do, then reward it like a child, encourage it, give it ten times what it needs.

Question: I had the impression that this work had given me a greater calmness in life. But I see that the periods of depression and exultation are stronger than before. I come to the point of not seeing things as they are. Too rosy or too black. How can I see things as they are?

Gurdjieff: Take a task, it does not matter what. Begin there and follow it to the end. And when you have accomplished it, take another.

Question: I have already taken one.

Gurdjieff: Well, take a more difficult one, if you have done a small thing. This task will help you to remember yourself. Take a task which serves as a factor for self-remembering. You have for instance, relatives, a father, a mother, a brother. Give yourself your word that you will direct them to do things which will sooner or later bring them to a different state from that in which they now are. You must do what is necessary to change their state.

Question: That means work to change my parents?

Gurdjieff: Any feature in them. For instance, with your brother, your sister, or your father; someone whom you see frequently. Even a servant if you like. It must be established in you in such a way that seeing this person, creates a reminder for you by association. Suggest to yourself that on seeing this person, it reminds you of your work. Then, you will remember automatically. Be it understood that you suggest to yourself good feelings towards this person. It is too easy to do evil. It is easy to suggest evil to another.

Question: I want to know something else; how long should one spend on exercises, on inner work, when one is alone at home? I want to know a basis of time, an hour, half an hour. How long?

Gurdjieff: There is a general rule; one should not work for more than a third of one's waking time. The other two-thirds should be spent in living automatically, as you are accustomed to. For the work, the other third; only that. Never more. Start from there. If you work for three hours you can spread them over the morning, the afternoon and the evening, but divide your waking time into three parts. Two for ordinary life, one for the work. That is the rule.

Question: If I work for four hours a day, I remain under the impressions of work, and I do not succeed in being as I was before, in finding again what I was before.

Gurdjieff: Play your role consciously. Internally, do not identify, externally play a role. This phrase which I often repeat is work. Internally, you cannot be as you were before. But like an actor you play the role of what you were before.

[Mr. Gurdjieff goes out of the room.]

Mme de Salzmann: No one has any more questions?

Question: I wish to know how one can see the quantity of the force that one dispenses in life?

Mme de Salzmann: Why that question? Ask the burning question of which you are in need.

Question: I tried to feel detached from others. When I am with a sick person I try to feel independent of him. To feel that I am not him, and I am not dependent on him. This does not prevent me from being to a certain extent dependent on him, if it is only to earn my living. I am obliged to have a special attitude. I see my financial dependence. Which means that I cannot feel at the same time my material dependence and my real independence.

Well then, this makes my relations with others impossible. It spoils my feelings of goodness, of real interest for others. Everything gets mixed. I prefer those whom I am not dependent on at all. If I were independent in life, it would be quite different. But this is not the case. I depend on my body. St. Francis did not feed his body. It was all the same to him—

[At this moment Mr. Gurdjieff came back and Mme de Salzmann translated the doctor's question.]

Gurdjieff: If you play your role, you feel free and you fulfil your obligations better. At the same time, internally you are more patient.

For instance with each person I am different. I am different with everybody. At the same time for me everybody is the same merde, the same stinkingness. Their emanations are equally bad, stinking. Well then, for you, your patients, your clients, all of them you must look at objectively, as nonentities.

It does not depend on them that you earn money. You can earn it just as well from others. You cannot make it at home. You take it for your exterior life. Internally you are free, you are yourself. You should be proud. He is perhaps not yet like you. There are millions of clients like him. You are alone in being as you are. This will bring you freedom.

Question: This does not prevent the fact that on a certain plane I depend on him.

Gurdjieff: No. If it is not he, it is another. It is clear. If it is not he, there are millions of others. You must not identify with this.

Question: Certainly I understand. But if I am free from him internally, externally I depend on him.

Gurdjieff: Excuse me. If you play your role consciously you are free. You are a doctor, you do what is necessary for him. Then if you do not identify, internally you are free. And if you play your role consciously, you are free. These two things go together. Do, do and begin again. How can one be dependent? I am not dependent.

Question: But this one who is in front of one, does he not feel that one is giving him nothing? Does he not expect a feeling that one gives him? Will he not feel the lack of this?

Gurdjieff [laughing]: This is for psychopathy. How can this nonentity feel? If she wants it, it is automatism, she imagines. It is merde. It costs nothing. No one can feel; it requires a special state. I know someone who is capable of feeling; but in order to feel he must isolate himself and prepare himself. He needs conditions. But like this no one can feel. Each man suggests to himself. You never understand either him or me. You understand what you suggest to yourself. That is psychopathy. You say to yourself, he is like this, he is like that, he is angry. But no, it is your own idiocy which suggests to you.

Mme de Salzmann: Is it clear to you? You do not understand another, you suggest to yourself.

Question: And if he hits me? I do not suggest this to myself, all the same, it is true.

Gurdjieff: It is your fault. You suggested to yourself. And you suggested to him. He would not have done it if you had not suggested to him.

Question: When I am with a sick person, and I try to see who he is, that he is nothing, and I do not depend on him, that he is merde, I experience pity. You would say: who am I to allow myself to experience pity? But if I try to play a role, that is to say to please him—because unfortunately it is the state of medicine that it tries to please the client. If I please him, well then I get the impression of sinking into his nothingness; and that—no—I cannot do. I cannot.

Gurdjieff: With regard to this, we have often spoken of justice. On one side there is justice, on the other egoism. The sick person is an object for my egoism. I have already had millions of patients like that. I looked at them as objects which I used in order to understand better. They interested me in order to increase my comprehension, they gave me elements for my knowledge. That which gives me knowledge is an object for me. I nurse him in order to cure him, but it is not he who interests me. I continue to learn, I make experiments. At the same time, I do not forget justice. I never do evil; I take care of him.

Look at it in this manner. You work for your experience, for the future. You can even experience pity. But look at him as an object. You can do this if you take as a task, to look at him as a field of experience. There are two sides; first to learn through him; secondly, internally not to identify, and externally play your role. There is a third side; in the future, you promise yourself to do better with the next person that you see. You promise yourself to do better tomorrow than today. If you do these three things well, you will get a quite different feeling.

Question: I think I should make real progress if I stopped being passive before everyone. Everyone is my master. I always give way. I have millions of masters, everyone I meet. How then could I become my master? I do not wish any more to be passive before myself and others, but to impose my will on others, to be active.

Gurdjieff: You must become yourself. Only after this is your work possible.

Question: How can I stop having this attitude whereby systematically and beforehand I accept whatever others impose upon me? For instance, to say no. I am incapable of doing this.

Gurdjieff: Excuse me, do not get angry, but for me, three sexes exist, masculine, feminine and intermediate sex. Excuse me, but from the beginning, you have been on the list of the third sex. There are five or six people like this, neither men nor women.

Question: Do I have to remain like this to the end of my days?

Gurdjieff: No.

Question: What shall I do? What I am looking for, is not to impose my will like a sorcerer, it is to impose my will on myself, so that I can be seen as I am, capable of answering yes or no.

Gurdjieff: I pity you. It is not your fault. It is the fault of your education; education of merde. Your society, your customs, the "what will they say?" They only give you exterior things.

[Mr. Gurdjieff tells of his anger, when he gives a sweet to a child in the street, and the father or mother obliges the child to say thank you, saying to him, "What does one say?"]

With you it has been like this. The result is extraordinary, neither man nor woman, but . . .

[Mr. Gurdjieff uses a Russian word which no one succeeds in translating, and which signifies "prostitute in trousers."]

If you wish to know what to do, come and see me.

Question: I have noticed that when I watch my breathing, I get better self-remembering. Should I do it?

Gurdjieff: If you think that there is a risk of this becoming a fixed idea, do not do it. If you think that it can help you, continue. You alone can judge.

Question: How shall I know if it is a fixed idea?

Gurdjieff: Now I have understood. If you had not asked this question, I should not have understood your interior state. What is the centre of gravity for your work?

Question: This exercise of the "I" and the one of seven respirations.

Gurdjieff: Which one interests you the most, which one gives you the most confidence?

Question: I do not do them in the same conditions, both are important for me.

Gurdjieff: Change the conditions in which you do the exercises.

The one which you do during the time of work, do in life and reciprocally. Change the times. I am afraid that you will automatise the times when you do them, that you will take habit, and that it becomes a fixed idea. In changing the times, you can perhaps avoid the fixed idea, and get a result.

Question: You told me that I lacked organic will. From where can I get this impetus which will give me an organic will?

Gurdjieff: Only one means can help you; you must suffer organically; for instance, not eat enough. Or this, your organism does not like the cold, endure cold water. The same thing with hot water. Do the opposite from that to which your organism is accustomed to do. Make it suffer. It will not be a psychic suffering. We have seven qualities of suffering; for us organic suffering is necessary: with your intellect you can direct your organism without mercy, force it to suffer. It is the unique means of getting this thing which you lack. In you two parts work, but not the organism. Have you understood your emotion? If you have constated, if you believe me, do this, struggle, suffer. Afterwards we will speak again. Then you will be capable of working on yourself. I am glad that you have come to this question by yourself.

Yahne: You gave me an exercise of self-remembering which consisted in feeling four points. It was very difficult at the beginning; now it is a strong feeling, but isolated . . . But my past fear, my timidity, my weakness have taken hold of me again. Should I continue this exercise, which, I have the impression, brings me nothing?

Gurdjieff: Do you have a suspicion why these things from your past have returned?

Yahne: As I suffer from much present confusion, I had thought that that exercise would help.

Gurdjieff: Do you begin to see what these weaknesses are in you which bring about this state of confusion? . . . If you ask me sincerely, continue this exercise a little longer, but this time I make an absolute condition, categorical. It is, to do it with a serious struggle. If you do it in this way, for a month, I promise you that after that, in one week, you will be rid of all your past misunderstandings. But that, if you continue . . .

Kahn: You told me a few weeks ago to be merciless towards myself. First I understood that it was necessary to impose harder conditions of life on myself. Then it seemed to me that little by little I understood more deeply, and that to be merciless towards myself is to struggle against three things: lying, fear, and having pleasure from myself. But I am always as if cut in pieces. It seems to me that what is good and what is bad in me balance each other.

Gurdjieff: There are three bitches—hope, faith, love, but a fourth is the mother of the three—it is Helena. It is like with a woman; if a man lets her have her own way, he becomes her slave, a bitch in trousers.

Kahn: I know that it is she that I must destroy, in order to become a man.

Gurdjieff: No, not destroy. You must do the same as with a woman; make her become your child. You must fight against egoism.

Kahn: For quite some time now I have not been led by egoism in my relations with my people.

Gurdjieff: But it is always there.

Mechin: I have the same thing to say about fear as "maître."

Gurdjieff: No. Yours is something quite different.

Mechin: I see this fear goes through all my manifestations. And its cause is a certain complacency towards myself.

Gurdjieff [speaking to Aboulker]: You see, doctor, these are quite different natures. In order to treat them, one has to take quite different measures. *[To Mechin]* Your grandfather comes from Auvergne; he is a Jew. There are subtle differences in the manifestations. Never take someone else's idea to make your question.

Mechin: I have tried to struggle against complacency, and I have partly suppressed the fear. But that is not enough. There is certainly something which I do not see.

Gurdjieff: Give birth in yourself to what you have understood with your head. Introduce it practically in your life.

Mechin: It is what I try to do.

Gurdjieff: It is organically that one must change. After that he will be able to continue our way.

Aboulker: Sir, I realise that I am incapable of taking a decision—absolutely incapable. I am not able to choose. I wait to be forced by life, then I adapt myself to the situation.

Gurdjieff: You must learn to come to a decision and to carry it out, and begin through little things. If you do not have great power you must decide on little things. It is a very important condition. One must have the corresponding state. It happens to you even now to have sometimes this state artificially.

It is necessary to keep aside two or three hours free. Relax yourself. Put all your attention, all your possibility, on relaxing the three classes of muscles. Further, when you have separated yourself, that is to say, the machine is one thing and the psyche another (without letting them fuse again) choose and decide. You have prepared a paper on which you write your decision. Continue to guard organically this state. Write down your decision and at the same time write down different remarks on your state. Then you can come back to your previous state. Forget what took place. For one or two days don't touch it. If you remember this state, try to remember the taste of it, but without thinking about what has been written. Then believe what you have written and stop believing in yourself. Your paper should be for you a holy image, your gospel, but remember that you are still small, and that you can only do little things. After you will be able to have faith in the future.

Aboulker: What torments me is my state of agitation. Truly, I think about the symbol of the wandering Jew. I never feel interior peace. And I would also like to ask Mr. Gurdjieff: I do not know how to read. Is there an exercise for learning to read?

Gurdjieff: You mean, to understand what is your form of disharmony? I will give you a page of Beelzebub, and you will take it as a task to read, beginning from the end backwards; then reread it the right way round . . .

Aboulker: I have been asking myself if I shouldn't do translations.

Gurdjieff: No. Not translations. In order to translate, one needs years of preparation. You will take this material in this page, and you will make an article or a lecture out of it.

Aboulker: I know that I have had this habit since my childhood.

Gurdjieff: Not only since your childhood. Since the childhood of your father and of your mother.

Pecquer: I have taken it as a task to play a role with my parents. I have taken it very seriously and for a long time. What I found out brought me a feeling of sadness which now hinders me from working. It is a weight which will trouble me all my future, unless I can overcome it.

Gurdjieff: You might say that you have remorse of conscience concerning your past relations with your parents.

Pecquer: No. I cannot say this, because I have seen that I am not responsible for what has happened.

Gurdjieff: The past—you must forget it. You are a responsible man and you must begin to pay for your existence. The first cause of your existence are your parents, father and mother. They are for you like God. As long as your parents live, there is no God. God only appears when your parents have died. God loves him who loves his father and mother. Why? Because he prepares a place for God. Now, without manipulation, if you begin to understand that it is necessary to pay, don't think any longer about the past. If it is bad, that's bad luck. But father and mother remain God for you. Be now a source of rest for them, that they may live peacefully. For twenty years they have been sufficiently worried and nervous through you.

They have a right to rest. You are obliged to become for them a source of rest. From one side, do everything not to make them nervous, and from another side everything that would make them happy. Make it as a task that your parents should love you with a real love. They can only love you if you incarnate their ideal. If your father likes stealing to be done well, you must learn to steal and to be a good thief.

Philippe: But, sir, this brings up very serious questions. What if to please her, I had to become something horrible, abominable?

Gurdjieff: Inwardly, one would have to hate her for that, but outwardly, one would have to do it.

Philippe: Outwardly, in front of her, but not in reality?

Gurdjieff: Of course. It is a criminal advice to create such things in a child.

Philippe: How to love parents if one must hate them?

Gurdjieff: You are obliged. It is your duty. Your individuality must do it.

Philippe: Because it is stupid to wish to correct one's parents—it is impossible.

Gurdjieff: It is possible when you are very strong. But *you* must only do your own duty. It is idiocy always to wish to change others when you can't change yourself. Inwardly, from one side, do your duty, from another side repair your past and prepare a better future.

Mme Dub: I can't come on Saturdays, as you permitted, because of my job. I have found an impulse for working in the daytime, but I find myself in trouble with the exercise of remembering myself, in the same difficulties as at the beginning. I fall asleep when I do the relaxing exercise.

[Mr. Gurdjieff tells Mme de Salzmann to go on with the reading.]

Mlle Tal: The teaching has caused to be born in me a kind of witness who observes me mercilessly and that impedes me greatly. I have to struggle against this witness. I cannot do self-remembering any more. I can't relax any more. I am in a state of absolute revolt.

Gurdjieff: Along with this witness, perhaps something else has closed up in you?

Mlle Tal: Yes. There's a struggle between two things. The witness makes me see to such a point what I am that I am disgusted. But I haven't any strength.

Gurdjieff: Is the wish to change at any price crystallised in you?

Mlle Tal: Yes. But not strongly enough. Before, I could. Now I can't.

Gurdjieff: You must work hard. Harder. In order to see what a nonentity you are. You feel that there exists a possibility of changing. You perhaps have the taste. To change is only possible thanks to hard interior labour. If you don't wish for it, you are wasting time. You must not go on.

Mlle Tal: But that's precisely what I wish to do.

Gurdjieff: Then work. Struggle, struggle.

Mlle Tal: My work is theoretical at this time.

Gurdjieff: Then struggle. You have understood that you are two persons. The result of your struggle will be a substance which will crystallise different factors in you for a real function of associations.

[Russian dialogue.]

Mme de Salzmann: Conscious associations.

Gurdjieff: You have mechanical factors. You are a machine. Now you can crystallise factors for conscious associations.

[Russian dialogue.]

Mme de Salzmann: Consciousness is a property of man without quotation marks.

Mlle Dol: You have advised me, in order to do the remembering exercise better, to hold out my arms and to watch against relaxing, principally in the nape of the neck. In my nape there are many "crackings."

[Mr. Gurdjieff is astonished at the word "crackings" and says to Mlle Dol. that she is using "slang expressions."]

And each time I go down into a layer of associations, deeper than before. Now I always come to the same layer which I don't manage to break.

Gurdjieff: Why break?

Mlle Dol: I wish to go deeper.

Gurdjieff: This isn't our aim. Associations cannot change. They only stop at our death. When your attention is consciously busy with something, it doesn't see them. This is a good example. Your associations go on more freely. But in this case, your consciousness is absolutely at a standstill. It doesn't note anything. During the day, it is the same thing. Your attention is occupied with a work which you have need of for your aim. If you do work consciously, if you do not masturbate, then associations will not disturb you. They exist for themselves. You can even formulate like this: the obstacle brought by associations is proportional to the degree of conscious concentration.

[Russian dialogue.]

Mme de Salzmann: They hinder you in so far as you are less concentrated.

Mlle Dol: Nevertheless, I always end by dreaming.

Gurdjieff: You do it too much.

Mlle Dol: Yes, I'm worn out.

Gurdjieff: I said in the beginning: make a programme. Work no more than eleven, twelve minutes. Sometimes, accidentally, you eat something that permits you to work one hour. Don't do it, you could break something. Don't use possibilities when they come along. For example, by chance you take coffee with me. This coffee stirs you up. You could work an hour. You should not do it. You should not use this force. Your programme is only eleven minutes.

Hor: Mr. Gurdjieff, in accomplishing my task there are moments when I fail, and when I suffer from having failed.

Gurdjieff: It's a normal thing. But you should have hope. Little by little, make grow the substance which I have. It will serve to crystallise in you the factors for being a real man. Struggle. Struggle without accepting anything. Do it as if it were a service for someone.

Hor: Yes, but even when I struggle like that, I do it with a predetermined aim; I fulfil a task. And I am sure that if I make one more effort, I would not succumb.

Gurdjieff: It isn't like that, you can relax. You can struggle consciously only in proportion to the energy you possess. You have batteries. If they are empty, you can do nothing.

Hor: Then, one mustn't struggle.

Gurdjieff: Eleven minutes, no more. The following week, eighteen minutes. We need the result, this substance. Later, we will be able to use it. Now you are empty. When you have it, I will give you an injection and it will be crystallised. You must have a real desire, a desire of all the centres. Not only with the mind. It is necessary to have a desire for real work with all your being. You are young. You must get accustomed to it little by little. Chi va piano, va sano. [Who goes slowly, goes safely.] These questions are not very desirable. All that fills my head. My head is already full of worries. Life is difficult at this time, and if my attention goes away to these difficulties, it cannot go to answering these questions.

Gurdjieff: Who wants to say something. How is the exercise going? It interests me to know what you have ascertained.

Mme de Salzmann: Who has ascertained something that might be interesting to the others concerning the exercise?

Gurdjieff: That can show who works, what? Horande?

Mme de Salzmann: Then do you want to say if you have something to ask? One at a time.

Gurdjieff: Then, if you have ascertained nothing, it is because you have not worked. If you have not worked, what have you done?

[Mme de Salzmann repeats.]

Masturbated. *[To Mme de Salzmann]* Can one say it? Even over against good taste?

Mme de Salzmann: Yes, why not, in this case?

Gurdjieff [to Shaeffer]: You have just arrived, perhaps you have something to say? Have you ascertained something?

Shaeffer: I ascertain a result in the first part of the exercise. Something turns up in each limb. What I don't know how to acquire is the inclination. When I feel something, it is imaginary. I have renounced all voluntary action. Before, I made effort with my head. I do it no longer.

Gurdjieff: Your head must be like a policeman. That is all. It must repeat to you all the time that you are occupied by this work. It must not go away.

Shaeffer: Then I wait for something to happen.

Gurdjieff: By means of sensation?

Shaeffer: Yes, rather than to manufacture artificially. Then, for me, "to exhaust," I do not see very well what that can be. I feel sometimes something which stirs. I feel it in the place where one pulls something. The second phase is more difficult. After, I know nothing to do about it.

Gurdjieff: The importance, at the beginning, is the sensation. Then, if you have contact with the sensation, if you verify how you feel, then, a second thing is important; it is the way by which you pour out. Up till now no one has spoken of this important question this way.

177

Edith: I have ascertained a greater need to relax in life.

Gurdjieff: If it is thus, you have the inclination. It is only when you relax consciously, and when your head retains its role of policeman, that the relaxation has value. If you relax generally, it is weakness.

Edith: I am conscious of being rather tense in general.

Gurdjieff: You must not relax unconsciously. Yet when you are in your state of awakening, you must relax consciously. When you sleep, everything relaxes without you; that has no value. It is your bondage.

Zuber: Sir, in this exercise, the difficulty for me is always the turning of the limbs. On the contrary the sucage and the flowing out are easy. I am happy to do it. The great effort is the beginning of the exercise. In life, I flow out generally much more vitality and force and I have something of a bent for the exercise and that I have very often, or else all is, on the contrary, mad, cacophonous, much madder than before. I made an ascertaining. It is the need, if I am in bed, of closing a circuit, by putting the right leg against the left, the right arm against the left.

Gurdjieff: How to close a circuit, how to understand? I tell you the same thing; do not give your head permission to wander.

Zuber: This is done without any will.

Gurdjieff: Then why verify it? Why speak of it? It is an obsession. This can only give you many chances of entering an insane asylum. You must never *do* unconsciously. Even half-consciously, I advise you. All or nothing. Between the two is only psychopathy, obsession. Never *believe.* Do not have confidence. You are a very weak person. If, during one moment, your centre of gravity is in your head, then if it moves to your plexus etc., it is masturbation. The conscious effort consists in giving the initiative to all your centres. That is activity. All the rest, it is material for being a candidate for insane asylums.

Zuber: In spite of what you have just said, I think that it is bound up with work.

Gurdjieff: I know not. But I know that that must not happen. Not yet. Expect nothing. Send the rest to the devil. For you, there exists only your exercise. Do it until you are entirely content. All these combinations and manipulations can come after, but not yet. One must not let oneself be carried away. It is a very dangerous moment.

On one side you have the strength to fix and something can enter forever into you. Then, you would be obliged to become my client and I can never do for less than three English zeros and there exists only one remedy to rule these things—hypnotism. *And I advise it not.*

[Godet speaks and Mr. Gurdjieff interrupts.]

Your question costs nothing. Wait. You do not come enough. You come here once in three months. Collect some material. For you this work is one thing among others. You disturb with your question. Here there is another degree of comprehension. What you say interests no one. These people make efforts for years and work seriously. With your question, you only cause disturbance. In this exercise, it is very important to understand the way by which can be made the inclination. This thing that you suck in with the air that you breathe. How? What is it? It is not your business. From the lungs you cause to flow this result. It must go from each side of the navel, without touching it. Then, below, these two lines unite and from there, that spreads itself throughout all the sphere of the sexual organs. You must feel the whole sphere.

With your thought, you must journey everywhere as if you were painting quickly. You circulate everywhere. From there, you go to the solar plexus in exactly the same way. You go up again from the two sides of the navel to a little forward of the sternum.

[Mr. Gurdjieff indicates the periphery of the solar plexus.]

Like this, under the skin. Through the back, one cannot transmit to the solar plexus. Then, always in front, from each side.

Now, in order to nourish the head. You start from the coccyx in leaving the bone sideways. To the left and to the right of the vertebral column, from two sides, the path goes up again to each side of the cerebellum to the brain.

[Mr. Gurdjieff indicates on Tchekovich the path to travel over (en partant), from each side of the vertebral column, to mid-buttock.]

To cause to flow in the vertebral column, you must first do an exercise in order to get accustomed to having the sensations of the Kundalini. You know what that is? We used to have there a tail, formerly. It is necessary to do this only as an exercise, to have the sensation of this spot.

Do the exercise from two sides, alongside of the vertebral column to the root of the head (the cervical vertebras). The vertebral column must be felt in the centre, the sensation must be equal from two sides. The density must be equal also.

These things are very important. It is necessary now to train oneself especially to feel and to establish a contact with this path. After, it will be easy for you to send something by these paths.

Parallel with this exercise, one thing is necessary. It is possible that someone obtains a result. But then this result is going to disappear. In order that it may continue to exist, one must do a special thing with the voluntary thought. At the beginning and at the end of each exercise, you must pretend, be compelled, to close again. Think that what you have done stays with you until the next time and that the next time you will obtain more. You must be certain that what you have is not sufficient. Then, consciously, you close again. Instinctively, you can feel it and already that will help you.

And it is desirable that you would remember to do nothing which might cause you to emanate a great deal. If you really want to accumulate this thing, you must have all the time a concentrated state, consciously, unconsciously, instinctively.

Something can be obtained then disappear. It never accumulates nor settles down. On the one hand, this comes and on the other this evaporates to the devil. Like the smoke of a cigarette.

It will even be very useful, in finishing the exercise, for each to pronounce his subjective prayer and ask his ideal to help him to guard this thing until the following exercise.

If by chance you remember, between two exercises, you can repeat your prayer. Then you will be inured. You shall be able to always remember. You shall even be able to succeed in making appear a factor of recall.

In general, it is necessary to create some automatic factors of recall. It is necessary for you to undertake this quality of work. It is very easy. For example, how do you sit down to the table? You have never ascertained with which foot you sit down. You observe, that there also, you have automatism. You will connect something with this automatism, for a reminder of your work. With each time that you sit down to the table, this thing will be able to act as a factor of recall.

Another example, when you wash, you take a towel. Look to see with which hand. See how you automatise. You will see that each time, you do the same thing. Do it consciously, take it with the left hand, instead of the right. In this manner you make a contact with your work, in order to self-remember. Another example: you dress in the morning. Which sock do you put on first? The right or the left? You have not noticed? Observe now. You find out that you begin with the left, always. Set a task: begin with the right. And connect this new way of doing with the recall of your work. Whether you wanted it or not, you are obliged to put on your socks. If you change the way of doing it, you self-remember. Then you find something else etc.

Then, you will be able, perhaps, to self-remember five minutes. Now, you can only do it one second. We try to arrive at five minutes. When you can do it, perhaps you will be capable of sending back this instrument.

[Silence.]

Gurdjieff: Speak. Talk about something. Speak of it. Fasten there. With Tchekovich, I have something to do.

Shaeffer: I understand well everything that concerns the conservation of concentrated state—but Mr. Gurdjieff would he want to explain more than that which is fixed in a limb?

Mme de Salzmann: For the moment the necessary thing is to feel the path along which something must move and that you grow familiar with the sensation of this path.

Lemaitre: There is no flowing in the different centres? Only the leg and the sexual organ?

Gurdjieff: It is the same thing. Tomorrow you shall do this exercise to the end. Gradually as you have need of it, you shall use this path.

Mme de Salzmann: It is for training, for exercising in feeling these passages. You must know how you can flow.

Gurdjieff: It is important to know these paths. Later we shall speak of stations and of forks. From here to there, there are three stations. From each station, one must go in one direction and not in another. If you go to the left, instead of going to the right, you can crush a dog or breathe the stink of a sewer.

Godet: Does the way of the solar plexus compromise the lungs and the interior of the chest? Or must one feel this passage?

Gurdjieff: The plexus is a sphere. We do not meddle with the organs. In the plexus there are many nerves of which the total constitutes a brain. Previously, all the collection was here.

[Mr. Gurdjieff shows the approximate height of the diaphragm.]

But we have degenerated. It is not quite dispersed. This is distributed in different places.

[Mr. Gurdjieff shows the circumference of the chest from the beginning of the neck, in back of the clavicle to a little above the sternum.]

Then we shall be able to study details. For example, one point is your appetite, another your love, another still, all your impulses. Like in an electric station. The commanding post of your internal life is there. It is like machinery.

Shaeffer: Mr. Gurdjieff speaks of ways for flowing. And in order to suck in, how does one do it?

Gurdjieff: Imagine that you take in air. Consciously, if you do it consciously, you feel that you suck in. It is the same occasion. Good breathing leads to better sucking in. Good sucking in leads to better breathing.

Mme de Salzmann: This is done all alone.

Shaeffer: All that one sucks in is concentrated in the lungs?

Mme de Salzmann: That mingles.

Gurdjieff: It is transformed at the same time. There are millions of things. Many details. It is much more complicated than your car. Feel the sphere only. Do not manipulate. Do nothing in the sphere. Concern yourself only with the way of one sphere in the other.

[Plaidge asks for details on breathing.]

Gurdjieff: You take in air. In expiring, pay attention only to the process of flowing. Respiration becomes automatic. Only the inhaling is conscious. I repeat again: get used to this; when I say consciously, this means that all initiative comes from the three centres. In the beginning, in order to do it better, feel the site of the three spheres and mobilise, feel that everything comes from there. Train yourself. Then, if you ascertain that you work only with one or two centres, know that this is not consciousness. There is only real consciousness with the same intensity in three places.

For example, here is an exercise: I am—when you say "I" you feel the three centres. When you say "am," you feel also the three centres but differently. "I," it is as if something stood up. "Am," it is as if, in the three centres [places] something sat down. This is an original explanation. Do you understand?

[Horande asks for explanation on the circumference of the sphere of the solar plexus.]

Gurdjieff: It is like in surgery.

[Mr. Gurdjieff shows the circumference of the sides. To the height of the diaphragm, the line descends on the stomach and remounts them to join the sides.]

Horande: Do the two lines remain in the sphere?

Gurdjieff: No. Only the sphere. I showed the circumference of the sphere. When it is entered, it does not matter much.

Lebeau: Do the two paths join each other before entering into the solar plexus?

Gurdjieff: No. They enter independently. Then they leave also separately. Like in a city. Two ways for entering, two ways for leaving.

Zuber: If there is something of bad contraction on one of the two paths, must one abstain from subduing the contracting?

Gurdjieff: Pay no attention to this. Do the exercise. Do nothing special for this.

Mechin: The shoulders must be left on the outside?

Gurdjieff: You pass along here only.

[Shows the path situated near the neck, a little above the clavicle.]

For the shoulder, it is the vertebral column. *There* is the command post.

Tracol: I can have the sensation of the solar plexus and feel that my sentiment is not there. At that time I would like to understand well what Mr. Gurdjieff says.

Gurdjieff: This is normal. If you have the sensation of your solar plexus, you have already mobilised the place of sentiment. It is occupied. You cannot feel it. You must not feel it except in having the sensation. If, from this place, you want to feel your vertebral column, you can re-experience the initiative from there, but cannot experience it. In order to experience it, it is necessary that the thing felt be calm and not function.

Tracol: Then, it is not possible that the three centres might be present when I have the sensation of the three localisations.

Gurdjieff: No.

183

Tracol: Then how can I be attentive?

Gurdjieff: One must have the sensation of three things. Either see them or feel them. The important thing is a contact. At each moment. You observe different forms of contact. One time, you feel. Another time you have the sensation. Either you might see, or you might guess at them. It is necessary that you be occupied all the time, that you occupy yourself with this obligation. If you want it, if you decide it, the part of you that you esteem is obliged to do. Otherwise, you punish yourself. If you do not do it, it is the fault of your individuality. You must educate your individuality. Refuse it that which it likes. Give it nothing. Oppose yourself in all things. For example, that which you do to the right, do to the left. Everything to oppose it. And your individuality can find itself in a very bad situation. Worse than prison.

Mme de Salzmann: There is no worse suffering.

Gurdjieff: It is difficult but useful.

CPSIA information can be obtained at www.ICGtesting.com
Printed in the USA
BVOW07s1905281114

377155BV00002B/138/P